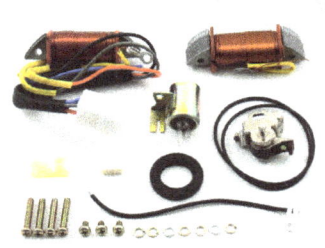

TBparts.com is the leading supplier of engine performance products for under 125cc 4-stroke Trail Bikes. We also produce a large line of high demand aftermarket replacement parts and vintage reproduction parts for popular models like the Z50 and CT70.

Please visit TBparts.com to see what parts we have to keep your mini on the trail!

Restoration Experts for both Z50s and CT70s

We can restore your Honda or build one to your specs and your budget.

Our restorations range from simply fixing your bike - to a 100-point restoration. We can paint in a factory color, or the hue of your choice. Honest and reliable – we have 15 years of experience making Honda owners smile.

We also offer:
Paint services
Parts & manuals
CALL US – we can build a bike that will take you back in time.

(208) 249-8020

Mikes MiniTrail Restorations
8959 New Castle Dr • Middleton, ID 83644
(208) 249-8020
Email: MikesMiniTrail@gmail.com

Honda 70 Enthusiast's Guide All CL, CT, SL & XL 72cc - 1969-1994

by Jeremy Polson

Published by:
Wolfgang Publications, Inc.
P.O. Box 223
Stillwater, MN 55082

Legals

First published in 2018 by Wolfgang Publications Inc.
P.O. Box 223, Stillwater, MN 55082

© Jeremy Polson, 2018

All rights reserved. With the exception of quoting brief passages for the purposes of review, no part of this publication may be reproduced without prior written permission from the publisher.

The information in this book is true and complete to the best of our knowledge. All recommendations are made without any guarantee on the part of the author or publisher, who also disclaim any liability incurred in connection with the use of this data or specific details.

We recognize that some words, model names and designations, for example, mentioned herein are the property of the trademark holder. We use them for identification purposes only. This is not an official publication.

ISBN: 978-1-941064-35-1
Printed and bound in the U.S.A.

Table of Contents

Preface 5

Acknowledgments 7

Dedication 8

0 - In the Beginning: DAX 9

1 - CL70 Honda Scrambler 15

2 - CL70 K1 Honda Scrambler 20

3 - CL70 K2 Honda Scrambler 23

4 - CL70 K3 Honda Scrambler 26

5 - 1969 Honda CT 70 29

6 - 1970 Black Tag Model CT - 70 . . 35

7 - 1970 H Model CT - 70 44

8 - CT70 1972 K1 and H K1 46

9 - CT 70 1973 K2 50

10 - CT - 70 1974 K3 58

11 - CT - 70 1975 K4 63

12 - CT - 70 1976 Honda 68

13 - CT - 70 1977 Honda 73

14 - CT - 70 1978 Honda 78

15 - CT - 70 1979 Honda 82

16 - CT - 70 1980 Honda 87

17 - CT - 70 1981 Honda 92

18 - CT - 70 1982 Honda 97

19 - CT - 70 1983-1986 Honda . . 101

20 - CT - 70 1991 Honda 103

21 - CT - 70 1992 Honda 107

22 - CT - 70 1993 Honda 112

23 - CT - 70 1994 Honda 117

24 - SL-70 1971 – 1972 Honda . . . 121

25 - SL-70 K1 1973 Honda 127

26 - XL-70 1974 Honda 131

27 - XL-70 K1 1975 Honda 137

28 - XL-70 K2 1976 Honda 141

Wolfgang Books Catalog 143

Preface

Everyone remembers his or her first mini bike, or if you were fortunate enough, your first Honda Mini Trail. If you did not have one, chances are you wanted one as a child. Pedal bikes were cool, but there was just something special about having an engine and the ability to climb hills and go fast that grabbed a kid's attention.

My love affair with the Mini Trail began in 1987 in the fourth grade. There was a Honda CT-70 for sale in the Duluth News Tribune where I grew up that caught my Dad's eye. The seller was asking $110.00 for it. My dad called on it being that he had one along with a Z50 as a kid, and was curious about it. My mom was against my brother and me getting a mini bike so that was as far as that phone call went. Little did she know I was dead set on getting a mini bike. After that one call, my grandparents dug out a box of family pictures and when I saw the picture of my dad's Candy Sapphire Blue 1971 Honda CT-70 I immediately fell in love with it. That was the mini bike I wanted to get and the color it had to be. I had never seen a trail 70 before in pictures or in person nor had I ever ridden a mini bike. However, in my mind I could not think of anything more fun to do than ride on the trails above my house after seeing those pictures. From that moment forward the hunt was on to find a CT-70 or at least see one.

It would not be long and for some reason or another I happened to be riding my bike around the neighborhood and I saw a hearse drive by with a blue CT-70 in the back, and yes, I did say hearse! My old hockey teammate's brother owned a hearse as a daily driver, my friend got a CT-70, and of all colors, it happened to be Candy Sapphire Blue! I can remember riding my bike by their house all the time just so I could look at it and admire the machine. I wanted one so bad! I can remember being out on a bike ride one time seeing my friend on the CT-70. Well, he ran out of gas and was pushing it home. I liked it so much

that I offered to push it to his house while he rode my bike.

After bugging my parents daily about getting a mini bike, it actually came to a point where it did not matter if they said yes or no because they were not easy to find. I posted a free want ad in our local paper every week for four years and finally after several summers of getting up at 6am to go take a paper off the paperboy's front porch with hopes of finding one in the paper we finally got a call. We went and looked at three non-running CT-70s for $300.00 and the person claimed that you could take all three of them and make one running bike. My dad was in favor of buying them because he knew how badly I wanted one. After he saw how bad they were and how expensive they were (at the time) I decided to pass and look for a better one.

I come from a family that loves collecting and each year my parents would travel to Red Wing Minnesota for the pottery convention. My brother and I would always stay with my Grandpa Harlan and Grandma Mary. When my parents returned, my Dad said that there was a Honda CT-70 in the Duluth News Tribune. When he called on the bike, the person explained that they had just had some work done on it at R.J. Sport and Cycle, the local Honda dealer. It was not but a few minutes into the conversation and I knew that we had seen it in the repair section at the dealership. They were asking $325.00 for the Mini Tail and my dad said he would buy it sight unseen. It was the summer of 1991 and I still own the bike to this day. The bike is a Mighty Green 1975 three speed CT-70.

Over the past 27 years, I have owned several hundred Mini Trails, sold thousands of parts, restored numerous show quality examples for clients, and continue to buy, sell, and trade on a weekly basis. Many people have come and gone in this hobby over the years, but it seems to me that every year I get a little deeper into it. When it comes to finding a rare, original low hour Mini Trail I am always in search of the Holy Grail, and that is what keeps me going. I was not born when the Mini Trail first made its way onto the floor at Honda dealers in the late 1960's. The baby boomers like my dad and uncle will look upon these pages and remember how much they enjoyed these bikes as kids. It's also all those kids that did not have their wish come true of owning a CT-70 when they were young. However, often times they are the ones that have helped the hobby grow. It is also for the younger generations that are starting to appreciate vintage motorcycles and are looking to be educated and take on this wonderful hobby. Whatever your connection was and is today, you are the collectors. You have a passion for collector motorcycles and a love for the Honda Mini Trail. This book goes out to all of you.

-Jeremy Polson

Acknowledgements

"You meet the nicest people on a Honda"

Not only do I love Honda Mini Trails, I always enjoy talking with people that are just as crazy, well almost as crazy, as I am about everything in the Mini Trail world. There are many people that I would like to thank for making this book possible, as well as for helping me out in the collector Mini Trail hobby.

My brother Chad Polson - my partner in crime, he has an eye for quality parts and always seems to find that rare Mini Trail or part. My grandpa Ron Polson for teaching me how to buy, sell, and negotiate. This passion rubbed off onto my brother and me and there is not a time that we get together that we are not talking about something with an engine. My uncle Bill Polson - he helped me acquire our first Mini Trail and his farm was our favorite place to ride growing up. My grandpa Harlan Behn, his truck has hauled more Mini Trails than I can remember. My friend Chris Langdon for being a major help in the restorations I did over an eight-year period. Chris shuttled parts and restored bikes across the country countless times, and has continued to play a part in this wonderful hobby.

I would also like to thank some of the great people that I have met over the years that have helped me out with my personal collection as well as making this book possible by providing pictures as well as documentation and information.

Brent Kolada of Virginia for providing photographs and documentation of his museum quality CT-70s. Lee Burry of Kentucky for providing photographs, documentation, and a wealth of information about the first model CT-70. Lee truly has a passion for first model CT-70s. Tim Lavoi of Minnesota: Tim has done engine restorations for my clients for over a decade and he does the best work on the planet hands-down! Art Jones of Minnesota for photographs and information on anything Mini Trail related. If Honda made it, chances are Art has owned it and probably sold it.

Jerry Ure Jr. of Michigan: Jerry has provided pictures, information, and parts and service. Jerry has painted countless frames for me and reproduced endless decals off originals I have provided. When I need a part whether common or rare, he seems to be able to come up with it. Ron Chiluk of Illinois: Ron is the master of carburetor restorations as well as brake plate and wheel hub restoration. Nobody has the knowledge and expertise for making old beat up parts look like the way they did when they left the Honda factory over forty years ago like Ron. The staff at Northeast Vintage Cycle has provided me with quality parts for client's restorations for over a decade. Randy Marble of Texas: Randy has allowed me to use photographs of various bikes to help make this book possible. Mark Mitchell of California-Mark has provided me with information on the early H model CT-70s and has helped build my collection by selling me some of the world's rarest Mini Trails.

David Gardner of Washington: David provided original sales brochures and original cycle test articles on the CL-70 and the CT-70. Jesse and Walt Kimball of Grand Marais Minnesota: Jesse and Walt spent a full day with me, shared their wealth of knowledge, and backed it up with an impressive collection of over eighty CT-70s. Scott Stewart at Stewart's Cycles & ATV, L.L.C: Scott provided photographs and information on the SL-70. Dennis Dillman of Texas: Dennis has provided photos and documentation of some of the lowest mileage 1st model CT-70s known to exist. Mike's Mini Trails for photographs of their low mileage 1982 CT-70. Bill Johnson for providing the opportunity for us to photograph motorcycles from his complete collection of CT-70s.

Gary Lewis of Michigan, owner of Vintage Honda Mini Trails. Gary has been in the Mini Trail business for over 35 years and has a wealth of knowledge, hundreds of original motorcycles; quality used parts, documentation, and one of the world's largest collections of NOS parts for 90cc and under motorcycles in the world!

If you are interested in contacting me about anything 72cc related from this book or about Z50 Mini Trails, I can be reached at jpolsonz50@gmail.com.

Introduction

After restoring several bikes, analyzing original bikes, and looking at bikes others have restored, I became fascinated with trying to figure out what parts actually came on particular bikes from the factory. After further investigations, I started to realize that there were many variations in particular parts just within one production year. It was at this point I gave up restoring Mini Trails for myself. I sold off all my restored Mini Trails and started hunting for original bikes in low-hour, unrestored condition. I enjoy restoring bikes and helping others find parts, but my passion is collecting original un-restored bikes. As the old saying goes, "you can restore them, but they are only original once". The purpose of this book is to cover the 72cc motorcycles from 1969-1994.

All of the information in this book comes from hands-on experience working with original Mini Trails as well as talking with fellow Mini Trail enthusiasts who have had similar experiences wrenching on original bikes over the years. I have provided the Honda recommendations for frame and engine serial numbers as a guide to let you know where Honda supposedly made the parts changes during production when possible. As you may have experienced, it is evident that these production figures are not always accurate.

Let the pictures, the engine numbers, the frame numbers, the literature, documentation, and my explanations help unravel the Mini Trail mystery. More importantly let this be a starting point, as I know there is much more to be discovered. It is my hope that this book will generate a lot of interest, get people talking, hopefully unearth some rare motorcycles, and most importantly, move the hobby to the next level.

Dedication

I would like to dedicate this book to my great grandparents, grandparents, and parents Rod and Sandy Polson. My mom got me interested in collecting at a very young age and my dad introduced me to the Honda Mini Trail over 25 years ago. The countless hours spent searching for parts, working on Mini Trails, and maintaining the ones my brother and I currently own are memories that will last a lifetime.

In the beginning…
DAX

In the early 1960s, Honda started with the "Monkey" bike. Near the end of the 1960s, another animal was introduced to the public, the "DAX". Dax is short for Dachshund or 'wiener dog.' The Dax name was a play on the look of the new series "ST" with its distinct "T-bone" hollow body frame, 10-inch tires, and fuel tank under the two-person seat. Officially released in 1969 as the "Dax Honda" ST70Z for general export, this completely new mini-bike kept with the Z50 tradition of being portable, but with a larger 72cc engine and frame. The original Monkey and Dax series of mini-bikes offered fold down handlebars, a detachable front fork, and two-fuel cut-offs.

A 1972 White DAX, also known by collectors as a Lady DAX.

A unique feature on the White DAX was the special seat with a green top and printed flower pattern.

The ST70Z model came with a 72cc semi-automatic three-speed engine. It came in two versions. Type 1 was a road-oriented motorcycle and type two was a dual-purpose machine like the CT-70 model sold in the USA. Type 1 had a low-mounted exhaust and metal frame decals like the prototype in 1968. It was also fitted with bigger "ducktail" fenders painted in silver. It was issued in three colors: candy ruby red, candy sapphire blue, and candy gold.

The second type had smaller, CT-70 style chrome fenders and an upswept exhaust. The decals were the familiar black/white stripe "Honda" version. The type two version was available in candy ruby red, candy sapphire blue, and candy special yellow. Both models had larger headlights with triangular-shaped speedometer and small chrome turn signals.

Honda also produced the Dax for the European market. This took longer because of differing laws and regulations for road vehicles in different countries. The first European Dax models were sold in 1970 and carried the K1 designation. In Europe, the Dax sold in two versions. Besides the ST70, there was also a model called the ST50 with a 50cc engine. This was because in many European countries the ST50 is considered a moped and the ST70 a motorcycle. One must be 18 years of age and licensed to legally ride a motorcycle in most EU countries. There are a number of small differences between the Dax models depending on the market for which they were intended. Tail lights, turn signals, headlights, mirrors, and such are mostly the same, but the biggest differences involve the German ST50 and ST70. The German type was equipped with the type one "ducktail" fenders but in combination with an upswept muffler, larger headlight, and a square shaped speedometer. The turn signals on the ST70 version were placed further away from the body and it was equipped with a chrome luggage rack. The tail light was round and colored half orange and half red. The special 49cc version was marked as ST50G (Germany).

In addition to the regular production Dax series, Honda also produced a special edition called the White Dax. Also known as the Lady Dax. This particular model came in ceramic white paint and had black/green/white decals. It also had a special seat with a green top with printed flower pattern.

Andrew Dell owns a 1972 ST70 White Lady Dax. JDM (Japanese domestic model). It is a rare four-speed model with hydraulic forks and a rotary engine. It is unique because most Lady Dax models looked like the CT-70 K0 models but this bike mimics more of the CT-70 HK1 model with the original flower seat. All warnings are in Japanese. How rare is this model? "I can only find one other person who has one like this (like the CT70 HK1)

Unlike the CT-70 K1 and H K1, the white DAX came with front and rear turn signals

Just like the CT-70 K1/H K1, the speedometer was separate from the headlight. The turn signals did not have long mounting arms like later models.

An early Honda DAX advertisement: Dax is short for Dachshund or 'wiener dog.'

A Rare Japanese Domestic Lady DAX owned by Andrew Dell. Unique features are the BMX style handle bars and the white paint marks on the front edges of the fenders.

Handle bar risers were used on this particular model to house the BMX style bars. The speedometer is in Km/H.

in the USA and only two others worldwide."

In 1972, Honda stopped selling the type one model and only sold Dax models with an upswept muffler and chrome fenders except for Germany where they kept the "ducktail" fenders. That same year the K2 model was introduced. Due to regulations, this version was limited to a speed of 45km/h or 28 mph. It had a governed flywheel, smaller carburetor, smaller intake, and milder cam.

From the introduction of the Dax through the mid-1970s, the little bikes kept getting better with numerous small running changes.

Although the production for the European ST70 and ST50 ended in the early 1980s, a Japanese version of the Dax, called the ST70M was sold in 1979. This Dax had a very distinct appearance with its megaphone muffler, 4-speed transmission, three spoke rims, lowered front fender and a chopper style seat with luggage rack.

Honda relaunched the Dax in 1986 with a few but significant technical improvements and designated it the AB23 instead of ST70. Now it had a 12V engine with camshaft supported by ball bearings, a hydraulic front fork and a chrome rear fender with a plastic mud flap. The upswept muffler was painted black and the heat shield had round holes like the CT-70. Bigger square plastic units on flexible shafts replaced the turn signals. This model was issued in three colors: Candy Ruby Red, Candy Sapphire Blue, and silver. The 72cc version was only sold in France.

In 1991, the first AB23 Dax was finally updated. This time a black painted engine, black muffler, painted fenders, white rims, and again new decals were present. It appeared in the colors Italian Red, Shasta White, and black. The red version was similar in appearance to the US market CT-70 of the same era. The main difference being the low-mounted fender and original-style folding handlebars on the Dax. The two models, which had evolved into distinctly different bikes, had finally come full circle at the end of the production run.

In 1996, the third and last generation of the AB23 was launched with some retro style improvements. It was once again equipped with chrome fenders, silver engine and rims, a black muffler & chrome heat shield. The colors were candy ruby red and candy sapphire blue. This model was produced until 1999 for the European market. During this time, the Japanese market had its own version, the AB26 Dax.

Despite its popularity, Honda ceased production of the Dax in 1999. Around this time, Honda's patents on the Dax expired and Honda sold the production rights to Jincheng, a Chinese motor manufacturer. (Dax history courtesy of Motor City Mini Trails of Michigan).

Above: *Most Lady DAX models have the first model CT-70 style forks. Very few are known to have the CT-70 K1 hydraulic front fork.*

Right: *Aluminum brake levers, black rubber grips, and a hi low switch like the black tag CT-70s were used on the White DAX.*

A center stand was standard equipment on this particular model, thus the need for the chrome grab handle on the muffler side of the frame

The speedometer was integrated in the headlight like the first model CT-70. Turn signals were also standard equipment long before the USA models.

A detachable front fork was used on this particular model.

Chapter 1
CL70 Honda Scrambler

Beginning serial number: CL70 100002

In 1969, Honda introduced the CL-70 Scrambler. 8,641 were produced in the first model year. The '69s, like most Hondas, have silver V.I.N. tags. Later in 1969, Honda added a black V.I.N. tag and motorcycles with those tags are considered 1970s. They are still first model CL-70s, or what some refer to as K0 models.

The CL70 was a spin-off of the CL90 and was a small motorcycle with the capability to go off road if need be. As a scrambler, it had a high-mount exhaust and a high rear fender. This allowed the look, though not really the capability, of extended off-road capability, before real dual-sport, motorcycles were available. The CL-70 had

*A first model CL 70 Scrambler with its
signature high-mount exhaust and high rear fender.*

a 72cc or 4.4 Cu in. four-stroke overhead cam single cylinder engine with a four-speed manual hand clutch. The transmission is a one-year only transmission for the CL-70 line up. The shift pattern is one down and three up whereas the next three models are four down. The frame is pressed together steel and came in Candy Blue and Silver or Candy Red and Silver. The front and rear fenders were both chrome plated. The front fender, like other street bikes hugged the front tire and had support braces on the outside of the fender and it attached to the inside of the front fork legs with four 6x12 hex bolts and washers. The left side of the fender had a chrome wire cable guide. This style fender was used through the K2 model. The rear fender, like the front was chrome and attached with four mounting bolts. The rear fender also had brackets for attaching the turn signals and well as a center mounting spot for the black rear number plate bracket/taillight bracket. The rear turn signals had round chrome turn signal bases with amber plastic round lenses. The rear taillight base was chrome and the lens red with a large reflector in the center. This taillight was used through K2 production as well as on other motorcycles like the CT90, CL90, CB750, and SL350.

The gas tank came in metallic silver with a one-year only chrome gas cap. The gas cap had no fuel shut off valve on top or any fancy designs. It was plain with knurling lines along the outside edge. Black rubber kneepads near the rear of the tank with a waffle pattern were also present. Round Honda winged badges with a white wing and the word Honda below it in raised chrome letters on an all-black background recessed into the tank and attached with two small screws. This emblem is a one-year only design.

The petcock valve had three positions on it, stop, on, and reserve. The petcock was aluminum and used on all four CL-70 models. The headlight bucket came in the main body color with a chrome headlight ring and a speedometer incorporated into the headlight bucket. The original Honda full-line sales brochure shows the headlight bucket in silver metallic like the gas tank so there may or may not be any floating around out there. The speedometer went up to 60 miles per hour and the numbers were in white on a black background. The numbers and hash marks were white with orange shift point lines for each of the four gears. The far left side was a green neutral light, the center red light was a high beam indicator light, and the far right was an orange turn signal indicator light. This headlight combination is a one-year only configuration as well. All '69 CLs came with front and rear spoked wheels mounted on 2.5-17 tires. Both front and rear hubs are aluminum and the spokes lace into

Round badges, black knee pads, and a ribbed vinyl seat are unique features to the first model CL 70.

them. The one-year only seat was black vinyl with eight heat pressed seams on top, a strap in the center of the seat, with piping around the edge of the seat. A silver Honda logo stenciled on the back of the seat.

The front fork had chrome uppers with chrome headlight bucket mounting ears, amber fork reflectors, long black rubber coil pattern fork boots with a chrome ring just below the boot, and aluminum lowers. The metal horn mounted to the lower triple tree on the front fork and the horn was used on all CL-70 models. A one-piece BMX style handle bar was mounted into two aluminum bar risers that sat on top of the silver metal triple clamp. The sides of the triple clamp had mounts for the turn signals as well. Two aluminum levers with black rubber tips controlled the front brake cable and the clutch cable. A gray throttle cable was also part of the cable assembly. Mounted in each lever were gray front and rear brake cables.

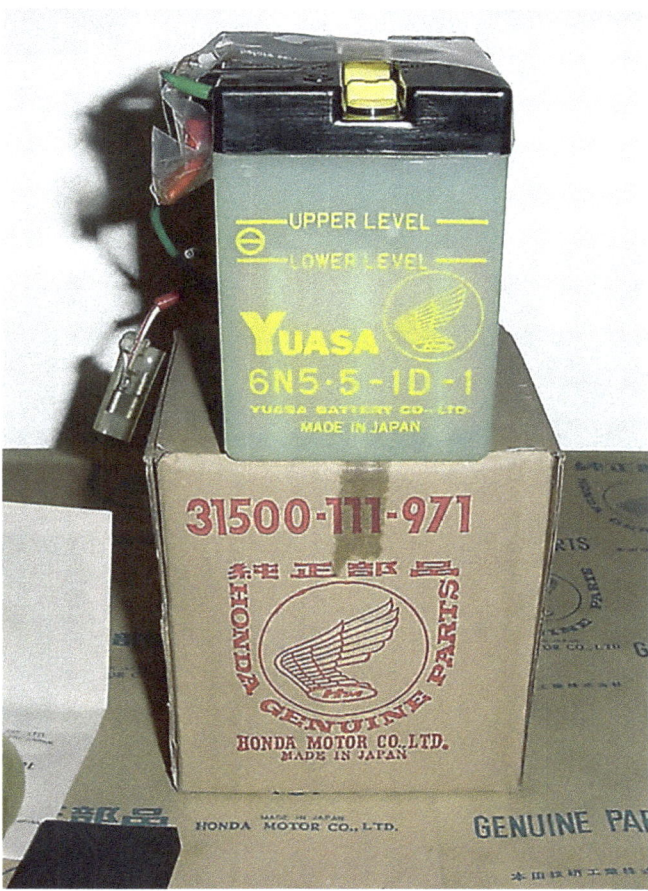

A new old stock green Yuasa battery with a Honda Wing on it. The Gary Lewis Collection

Chrome emblems with red paint and a "70" insignia in chrome. A full chrome slotted high-rise muffler.

Each side of the bar was equipped with two aluminum control switches. The left side black slide switch controlled the turn signals and had a black horn button. The right side switch was a dimmer control switch and it held the gray front stop switch. Both control switches had threaded holes for left and right chrome mirrors. The handgrips were black with small ribbed lines in them and very small donuts on the control sides to keep the riders hands in place.

The rear shocks are a one-year only item. They came with aluminum uppers, chrome shock coils, and aluminum lowers. Just like the frame and the headlight bucket, the rear swing arm was painted to match those components. On the kicker side of the swing arm was a muffler-caution decal in silver with black text. Rear buddy peg mounts were present in the swing arm and with the size of the seat it was meant for riding double. Underneath the black knee pads on the sides of the gas tank were chrome emblems with red

Braced chrome fenders, spoke wheels, and long black rubber fork boots were present on all 1st model CL-70s.

paint with a "70" insignia in chrome. The four-speed 72cc engine came in all silver metal finish, unlike the CT-70, which has a black cylinder. The right side of the engine had an aluminum clutch cover with a polished aluminum clutch adjustment cover. The left side of the engine had a split flywheel cover to fit around the rear swing arm. It also had a removable points cover with "Honda" in the center and "Made in Japan" along the bottom.

To protect the chain, a chrome chain guard with four decorative indented circles in the front half of the guard was used. A 47-tooth rear sprocket was used. On the shifter side of the frame a black knob was present to remove the side cover and get at the battery that was connected inside the frame. The battery used on this model is a 6N5.5-1D-1. The kick-starter was chrome with a curved bend rather than being straight like the CT-70 kick starter arm. It had a black ribbed rubber for limited slip while kicking over the motorcycle. Below the kicker was a chrome foot brake pedal with the rear brake rod linkage hidden behind the rear swing arm. Below the engine was a black step bar with large rubber foot pegs for added grip. The motorcycle could be worked on, displayed, or propped up for everyday parking using the black double-legged center stand assembly. The carburetor was exclusive to

A Nippon Seiki 60 mph speedometer integrated in the headlight bucket.

the first model CL-70. It used a large rubber tube called a "muffler" that fed into a black plastic air cleaner cover that mounted under the seat. This air cleaner system is arguably one of the most complex systems out there.

One of the most noticeable features on the CL-70 that helps give it the "scrambler" name is the exhaust system. The exhaust system was upswept just about the crankcase and slightly horizontal. A large solid chromed out muffler with one lower chrome heat shield and one large chrome upper heat shield outfits the motorcycle. All CL-70s have a muffler drain tube. In order to mount the muffler by the top of the rear shock a muffler stay bracket is used and it is painted to match the frame. On the left side of the motorcycle is an ignition switch mounted in the frame. The same key also works the fork lock that mounts at the bottom of the fork just below the ignition switch.

A one-piece BMX style handle bar mounted into aluminum bar risers. A one year only gas cap. The left side switch controlled the turn signals and had a black horn button. The right side switch was a dimmer control switch and it held the gray front stop switch. Both control switches had threaded holes for left and right chrome mirrors.

Chapter 2
CL70 K1 Honda Scrambler

Beginning serial number: CL70 200002

In 1970, Honda produced a second model of the CL-70, a K1 model. Sales were better than the previous model, 14,061 were produced. Many of the features remained the same as the previous model, but like most new model motorcycles, the 2nd model usually undergoes the most changes once the bugs are worked out.

The transmission was one of those changes, even though it was not a cosmetic change. The transmission shift pattern went from one down and three up to four down and this pattern would remain the standard for the remaining production of the CL-70 line. Two colors were offered for the K1. Candy Topaz Orange and Candy Riviera

Candy Topaz Orange CL 70 K1 with a Silver Metallic tank. New for 1970 was a separate speedometer from the headlight bucket.

Blue. Both Motorcycles had Silver Metallic fuel tanks with stripes going over the top of the tank that matched the main body color. A new chrome gas cap was used on the K1 and it would be used until the end of CL-70 production. The headlight bucket as well as the swing arm also matched the main body paint. The fuel tank no longer had the black rubber kneepads on the sides and the emblems were switched to durable stick on emblems. The top emblem was the signature Honda wing with the "HM" insignia at the bottom of it and the "Honda" logo below that. Both emblems were black with silver outlines.

Two major changes that took place were the seat and the headlight and speedometer configuration. The strap was eliminated from the seat and the upper pipping was switched from black to white. Ten heat pressed seams are present on the top of the seat cover. The headlight bucket for the remaining production of the CL-70 lineup did away with the speedometer and headlight bucket configuration. Like many other Honda motorcycles, Honda mounted the headlight bucket inside the fork ears and mounted a speedometer bracket on the top of the triple clamp to hold the speedometer. Not only was the speedometer configuration different, but the speedometer was different as well. The speedometer was a black canister type of speedo with chrome around the bottom edge. The face of the speedometer was black

Candy Topaz Orange CL 70 K1 with a Silver Metallic tank.

All new stick-on Honda Wing tank emblems. A fork lock was present and the ignition switch is mounted on the shifter side of the frame.

The rear shock top covers were added for 1970 and they matched the paint color of the frame. Chrome chain guard and 47 tooth rear sprocket.

with white numbers. The speedometer had a top speed of sixty miles per hour. It had four orange shift points below the miles per hour marks. There were three indicator lights in the speedometer. The far left one was green for neutral, the middle one was red for the high beam light, and the far right was orange for turn signal notification. The bottom of the speedometer said "Nippon Seiki Japan".

New for the K1 were rear shock covers. The tops of the shocks received body painted shock covers like many other motorcycles in the Honda lineup. The wire harness, coil, and ignition switch were changed for the K1 and they were used through the final CL-70 model. The rectifier and battery were the same for all four models. The muffler was used on the first three models and the upper heat shield was used on the K1, as well as the previous model. The lower heat shields on the muffler are unique to the K1 and K2 CL-70s. The upper heat shield is used on the first model as well as the K1 model. The battery cover emblem and opposite side emblem remained the same as the previous model.

2.5-17 tires mounted on spoked chrome wheels.

Chapter 3

CL70 K2 Honda Scrambler

Beginning serial number: CL70 300002

In 1971, Honda built the K2, or the third model of the CL-70 Scrambler line. Sales were slightly down from the previous year. 13,700 were produced. New for the K2 model was the addition of having three-color choices compared to two the previous two model years. The K2 was the only CL-70 to offer three-color options. The color choices were Candy Sapphire Blue, Candy Red, and Candy Topaz Orange. All three colors like the previous models came with the frame, swing arm, muffler-mounting bracket, rear shock covers, and headlight buckets in the main color. New for 1971, the upper fork ears also came in the main body color.

Candy Red K2 CL 70. The only year Honda offered three-color choices for the CL 70.

Four chrome buttons on the bottom sides of the seat, K2 only.

Silver Metallic fuel tank with a large upper stripe and a thinner lower stripe in the main body color.

The gas tanks all came in Silver Metallic with a large upper stripe and a thinner lower stripe in the main body color. The gas tank emblems were the same as the previous model year. The battery cover emblem and opposite side emblem were changed for the K2 model. This time the emblem said "CL" in yellow and "70" in white with a black background outlined in silver. The seat made significant changes. The bottom of the seat had four buttons along the front bottom edge on both sides. Just above the rear shock on each side of the seat, white pipping curved up and wrapped around the top back of the seat. The top of the seat had nine straight heat pressed seams and a tenth seam that curved around about an inch from the very back of the seat. The seat cover was black with a silver "Honda" logo across the rear center of the seat.

The muffler underwent some changes. The upper heat shield was all-new for the '71 K2. It had multiple vertical cutouts in it with three sections of horizontal cutouts in a pattern from left to right of two, four, and three. The muffler itself was used on all first model CL-70s as well as the K1 & K2 models. The front and rear lower heat shields were used on all K1 and K2 CL-70s. The rear fender blinker assembly, and tail light assembly was used on the previous two models and the K2 was the final CL-70 to use these parts. The rear shocks, chain guard, foot brake, center stand, foot pegs, front fender, handle bar, control switches, speedometer, flywheel cover, battery, front fork, headlight, petcock, kicker, shifter, and wheel assemblies were the same as the previous model year. The carburetor was the same as the previous model year and was used K1-K3.

The final model to use this style rear fender blinker assembly and tail light assembly.

The upper heat shield was all-new for the '71 K2. It had multiple vertical cutouts in it with three sections of horizontal cutouts in a pattern from left to right of two, four, and three.

Chapter 4

CL70 K3 Honda Scrambler

Beginning serial number: CL70 1300001

Nineteen seventy-two marked the final model of the CL-70 and it was produced and sold into the 1973 model year. The K3 made several changes making the final CL-70 motorcycle a special one. The color options for the K3 were Candy Sapphire Blue and Candy Ruby Red. Both colors came with a "special Silver Metallic" gas tank with a black and red pinstripe around the black/silver "Honda" emblem.

The battery side cover emblem and the opposite side of the frame emblem are the most decorative emblems in the CL-70 lineup. The emblem said "CL" in black with a chrome outline. Then it said "70" in red outlined in black with a little bit of chrome between the two colors. Below the "CL 70" script was

The final CL 70, a Candy Sapphire Blue example courtesy of the Todd Evans collection.

a diamond emblem in red with a chrome border with the signature Honda wing in the center in chrome. The battery-cover black twist knob latch was used again and was used on all other CL-70s built. The rear swing arm and rear shock covers came in the body color. New for the K3 was the headlight bucket and fork ears in something other than the body color. The fork uppers and headlight ears were chrome and the headlight bucket came in black. To go with the new fork design a new style of fork reflectors was added as well. They were large and were intended for safety. The fork boots were a K3-only item. The K3 fork boots had more accordion lines in them than the previous three model years. The previous model years each had ten accordion lines in the boots. The front turn signal bracket remained the same as the previous three models.

For the fourth model in a row, Honda changed up the seat design yet again. Like the previous three models, the seat was black with a silver "Honda" logo on the rear center of the seat. The seat had three chrome buttons along the bottom front edge where the driver sits. The rear sides of the seat had heat pressed seams connecting the side vinyl to the rear vinyl. The top of the seat had 19 heat pressed seams from front to back. The biggest change for the K3 was the complete exhaust system. The muffler is a one-year only part; it was only used on the

A "special Silver Metallic" tank and headlight bucket and a new three button black vinyl seat.

A "CL" in black with a chrome outline emblem with "70" in red outlined in black with a little bit of chrome between the two colors. A diamond emblem in red/chrome with Honda wing logo in chrome.

A one-year only muffler with a "CT-70" porthole type of upper heat shield.

All new front and rear fenders, K3 only.

K3. The lower header pipe shields were a one-year only combination and the upper heat shield was a one-of-a-kind as well. The upper heat shield looks very similar to the heat shield used on the K2 model CT-70. The upper heat shield on the CL-70 was chrome with six large portholes. The face of the heat shield around the portholes was high-heat black paint. The front portion of the heat shield had thirteen vertical louvers cut into the shield for airflow.

To go with the redesigned exhaust system was a chrome muffler-mounting arm that attached to the rear shock. The coil, rectifier, and battery were used on all CL-70s. The wire harness, carburetor, complete wheel assemblies, handlebars, hand grips, levers, clutch cable, throttle cable, speedometer, step bar, center stand, foot brake pedal, silver swing arm warning decal, the turn signals, complete air cleaner assembly, and the rear shocks were the same as the previous model year. New for the 1973 K3, on the back of the left side of the frame was a helmet lock that used the ignition key. The front and rear fenders were a new design as well. With the new design came the other parts to complete the changes. The taillight, license plate bracket, and the turn signal mounting assembly were K3 items only. Unlike the previous three model years, no production numbers have been reported for the final CL-70.

Chapter 5

1969 Honda CT 70:
The Mini Trail's Big Brother

Engine serial number beginning and ending: CT70-100001
Frame number beginning and ending: CT70-100001

After one year of production for the Honda Z50A Honda was ready to expand its Mini Trail line-up, and they hit a home run with the CT-70 Mini Trail. June 26th 1969 was the official release date for the 72cc Mini Trail. The first CT-70 came with a three-speed automatic transmission with a downshift pattern. Like all 1969 motorcycles produced by Honda, a "Silver Tag" was installed on the front steering head tube, without build date or model year information. 1969 CT-70 production only ran from late June until the end of August. Honda started adding black identification tags with a month and year date in the top right corner of the V.I.N. tags in September of 1969 and they are

Think black twist knobs, Phillips head chain guard screws, black plastic brake levers, non-removable points cover flywheel cover, and a stitched rear seam seat present on this Silver Tag example.

Silver Tag high beam light composed of a thinner material than later model lights. Prone to fading.

considered 1970 models.

The first serial number for a CT-70 is serial number 100001. The highest recorded Silver Tag serial number is 115493, a blue Silver Tag owned by Lee Burry of Kentucky. The lowest recorded serial number for a black identification tag 1970 model CT-70 is serial number 115598. The serial number range between the highest recorded Silver Tag and the lowest recorded Black Tag is 105 bikes. For the sake of argument, it is safe to say that around 15,500 Silver Tags were produced in just over two months of production. Some like to say that the Silver Tags were prototype motorcycles. Yes, they were the first CT-70s produced but they certainly were not a prototype motorcycle, but rather just a 1969 version of a motorcycle that spanned three calendar years with two models.

What makes the Silver Tag unique and desirable to collectors? The overwhelming amount of variations that the first bikes have compared to the 1970 and 1971 versions of the first model, are what make it desirable. What is interesting is the fact that some parts changed a couple of times within the Silver Tag run and some of the parts continued into the Black Tag run. It is hard to pin point when a particular part came and went but I will highlight the variations for enthusiasts to make note of when looking over their own Mini Trails.

The most notable variation that collectors look for when they come across a barn find is the Silver Tag V.I.N tag. The Silver Tag on the neck is from the same material as the Black Tags and there is no date of manufacture. As stated earlier, all 1969 Honda Motorcycles had silver front head-tube tags. The wheels have no bosses and the hub spokes are flat in the center and have circle marks on the shifter side of the hub. The hubs are one Silver Tag variation that do not span the entire run. The hubs made a change somewhere between serial number 107416 and 108481. A Candy Gold, Silver Tag, with serial number 109165 has the later style hubs. Lee Burry's high number Silver Tag does not have the early hubs. The headlight ring does not have as much detail around the adjusting screw as the Black Tag models do. The most notable variation is that the headlight ring is welded together at the bottom and later models are a one-piece unit. The high beam light in the speedometer is made of fabric rather than a lens. Inside there is only one rubber tube holding up the faceplate.

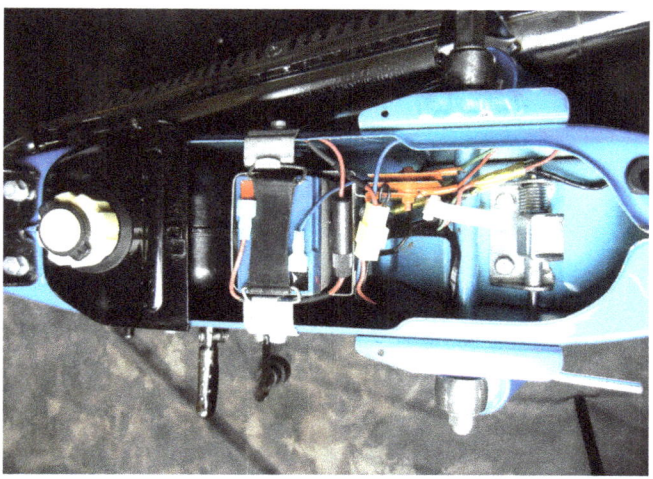

Early frame with taillight grommet hole for wire to go through. Early battery tray with rubber pucks, no plastic battery tray.

Like the Z50A K1, black plastic levers were used instead of aluminum hand brake levers. The engine cradles have square pads where the spark plug guard mounts onto the crash guard instead of rounded corners. Like the plastic levers, this variation actually ran into the 1970 model as well. The seat bottoms have three nuts and three bolts holding the tool kit compartment onto the seat pan. The seat cover had overlapping stitch seams on the rear sides compared to precise heat pressed seams on later versions of the seat. This version of the seat ran beyond the Silver Tag run. The tail light wire goes up thru the hole in the frame close to where the taillight mounts. Early taillights had brazed on connectors. The rear brake arm is straight and does not have any bends in it. The chain guard is held on with Philips screws and washers rather than bolts and washers for most of the Silver Tag run. Lee Burry has provided a Candy Ruby Red with serial number 111498 or the 11,498th CT-70 having Phillips head screws and a Candy Ruby Red with serial number 114449 or the 14,449th bike with bolts and washers.

Black rubber plugs were used to plug the holes for the chrome side stand handle used on the DAX model.

Most people, if they are even aware of it, believe there are only two chain guards used on the first model CT-70, when in fact there are actually three. The Silver Tag bikes used two different chain guards and the Black Tags used one. The early chain guard is a two-piece unit whereas the later chain guard is one. The first version of the chain guard has a straight bottom left corner whereas the second version of the two-piece Silver Tag guard has a

Silver tags used "NGK" spark plug caps. The early engine guards had square mounting tabs.

Hash marks and diamond marks are common on early CT-70 engines. Markings vary.

Early flat hub spokes with circle casting marks.

rounded bottom left corner like the Black Tags and the K1-79 models. The horn is black on the back and has screws holding it together. The muffler has a shotgun exhaust with a taper at the end instead of a stub diffusor.

A one-piece Z50 style stator/flywheel cover was used instead of a removable points cover type of magneto cover. The wire harness guide on the frame is silver and not black. This is easy to remember when authenticating a bike because the wire harness guides match the V.I.N. tags in color. The gas tank bracket is a little shorter than the later model brackets. This variation ran past the Silver Tag production. Large number-eight bolts were used to hold the wheels to the hubs. The rest of the motorcycle also used large number-eight bolts as well. The center bracket that holds the exhaust is different on a Silver Tag and possibly used on early Black Tags as well. It is a little larger and has a dogleg in it so it reaches closer to the frame. There is not an extra-long nut on the engine mount where it bolts on; instead, it has a short nut on the motor mount, then the bracket, then a lock washer and another nut. An NGK spark plug boot like the 1968 Z50A and early Z50A K1s was used. Later in the run, Honda made their own.

Contrary to what many believe, only the early engine bolt-heads have diamonds and hash identification marks. How many hash marks each engine has is a mystery as there is no rhyme or reason on the amount. Frame/engine 100261 has one diamond and two hash marks and serial number 101426 has one diamond and three hash marks. Brent Kolada's Candy Sapphire Blue Silver Tag with serial number 106095 has one diamond

Bridgestone and Nitto tires were used on Silver Tags. Early models used "Big 8" bolts.

and three hash marks. Brent Kolada's Candy Ruby Red Silver Tag with serial number 102022 has one diamond and one hash mark. Later in the Silver Tag run, the heads switched over to a letter and number casting. The common letters used are an "E" or an "M" and the number is a single or double-digit number. Lee Burry provided me with photos of a Candy Gold Silver Tag with frame number 108481 and the head is stamped "E 47". Lee owns a Candy Gold CT-70 with serial number 109165 and the head is stamped "M 1". Lee's Candy Sapphire Blue with serial number 115493 is stamped "M 3".

The early style air boxes did not have a rear rubber boot but rather a metal boot instead. The carburetor has aluminum fuel line connections that connect at a ninety-degree angle instead of brass fittings. The carburetor is stamped AT70A. This particular carburetor used the tall cap on top of the carburetor. The drain plug comes out the back of the carburetor and black line was used. No battery overflow hole was present above the rear fender. Thinner handle bar knobs were used and they were used into the Black Tag run. The front fender has a plate spot-welded to the bottom and it has a

Thin handlebar twist knobs and early Silver Tag speedometer integrated into the plastic headlight bucket.

Headlight ring welded together at the bottom. Early lip front fender and black backed horn with screws holding it together.

lip on the front edge and not a folded over safety edge like the later style front fenders. The early rear brake cable had a huge black rubber boot. To a novice collector it looks reproduction. A second version of the Silver Tag rear cable was made with a standard size rubber boot. This is one of the most unknown features of the early Silver Tags and Gary Lewis has one of each variation of the cable on his two early motorcycles. To secure the cable guide to the front fender, the front fender has nuts on the back. Honda used 5mm nuts and lock washers, not welded on nuts. (Note: there are cross-over front fenders that cross over between the Silver Tag and Black Tag. The cross over fender has no front lip but it has the nut/lock washer set up.)

No inner heat shield was used on the lower head pipe on bike number 101426, however 100261 has two heat shields. You might ask yourself, why did Gary Lewis' later Silver Tag have only one heat shield and the earlier one had two as all of the modern CTs have? This is possible because not all early parts ended up the early motorcycles. This is

Candy Ruby Red Silver Tag owned by Bill Johnson.

Gray T.S.K. cables and black plastic hand brake levers.

because parts were produced in batches and grabbed and put on motorcycles as they came down the assembly line. This proves that not all early bikes necessarily had the earliest parts. What it does prove is that more than one variation existed in the earliest stages of production.

One early Silver Tag parts change that occurred was the front muffler stay bracket. According to the Honda parts books only the first 2,874 CT-70s used the early bracket. A plain horn button without any T.E.C letters written on it was used on the first model. The first CT-70 axles produced required a standard axle nut and later they switched to a castle shaped nut that required a cotter pin to be pushed in and folded over inside the axle. This change took place at serial number 226905. Every CT-70 after 226905 used the castle nut and cotter pin. Clear line was used on the battery for overflow. Nitto tires and Bridgestone Trail Wing tires were used on Silver Tag models. Frame number 100009 with engine 100010 came with Nitto tires. The 1969 CT-70 came in three colors. Candy Sapphire Blue, Candy Ruby Red, and Candy Gold. For many years people believed that the first color off the line was Blue, and then came Red, and finally Gold. Frame number 100009 is gold so that begs the question, were the first ones gold or were all three colors made in the first ten produced? Whatever the case may be, all three colors were present in 1969. Gary Lewis of Michigan owns frame number 100040 and it is Candy Sapphire Blue. He also owns frame number 100261 and 101426 and they are both Candy Sapphire Blue. Serial number 101861 is Candy Ruby Red and Frame number 114389 is Candy Gold.

Early shot gun exhaust with a taper on the end instead of a longer stub diffuser.

Chapter 6

1970 Black Tag Model CT-70

Engine serial number beginning and ending: CT70-100001
Frame number beginning and ending: CT70-100001

In September of 1969, production continued with the CT-70, however by this time all Honda motorcycles came with a black V.I.N. tag installed on the front steering head with the serial number and the month and year the motorcycle was built. Like many motorcycles in the Honda family, parts were used from the previous year or model. Some were used until the previous models parts were used up and the new parts were phased into production. The CT-70 is a perfect example. In July of 2017, Lee Burry of Kentucky purchased a Candy Ruby Red "Black Tag" CT-70 from the original owner and it had all of the parts that a late Silver Tag would have. The serial number

Candy Gold unrestored black tag owned by Brent Kolada.

Type II seat with heat pressed rear side seams

All black tag frames and all silver tag frames at serial number 104866 and above have a frame brace between the top engine bolt where the air cleaner breather tube mounts.

is 116351. Art Jones of Minnesota has owned hundreds of CT-70s and one particular motorcycle is a perfect example of a "cross-over" model. His Candy Gold with serial number 122451 with a build date of October of 1969, a month into the new model year had plenty of the left over Silver Tag parts. The three-bolt early seat, the flywheel cover without the removable points cover, the square tabs on the engine crash guard, and the hole in the top rear of the frame for the taillight wire.

Because of the build date, it did not have the early carburetor. The brass fittings on the carburetor were present on this motorcycle. This particular carburetor is stamped AT7B and has brass fittings for the reserve line and the regular "on" gas line. The fuel lines were black rubber and the overflow line was black. The overflow line came out the bottom of the carburetor. The AT7B carburetor also came in a version where the drain plug fitting came out of the back and the gas reserve lines had large brass barrels that pushed into the carburetor, and the brass outlet tubes were connected to those. Two different carb tops were used on the Black Tag model CT-70; a tall carb top, and a short carb top as the ones used on the Z50A.

Brent Kolada's two Candy Gold CT-70s purchased together on July 8th 1970 with serial numbers 160676 and 160805 both have the large carburetor top like the Silver Tag models. His Candy Gold with serial number 165913 has the small Z50 style carburetor top. Based on the serial number ranges, the carb top change over took place during the 160676-165913 serial number range. The on/off twist knob on the first model CT is exclusive to this model.

Eventually the Silver Tag parts were phased out and the new parts were put into production and used until the last three-speed CT70 rolled off the production line in 1970. As stated earlier the seat cover eventually made a change on the rear side seams and the seat pan changed. The tool kit compartment was spot welded to the seat pan instead of being bolted with three bolts. The wire harness holder that attached to the frame outside of the engine crash guard was switched from silver to black. The tabs on the crash guard that hold the spark guard switched from squared corners to rounded corners. Honda started using their own spark plug caps with an "HM" logo on them instead of the NGK caps. A one piece stamped chain guard was used and it used bolts and washers instead of Philips head screws. The one-piece flywheel cover switched over to a cover with a removable center points cover. The front fender had a rolled over edge along the front and the side of the fender had threads in it to attach the cable guide.

Aluminum levers with black rubber tips replaced the black plastic levers; however, this did not take place right away. Brent Kolada owns three Candy Gold CT-70s in the 160805-165913 serial number range and all three have black plastic levers. Two of the CT-70s were purchased together from Knowles Sales & Service of Gunnison Colorado. The Honda parts books state that all CT-70s below serial number 186005 came with black plastic levers and all CT-70s with serial number 186005 and above came with aluminum rubber tipped levers. Todd Evans of California owns a Candy Ruby Red CT-70 with 478 miles on it. It was manufactured in April of 1970 with frame number 179812 or the 79,812th CT-70 produced. Based on the four, documented low mile CT-70s that fall below the Honda serial number range for black plastic levers, it proves that the levers were used on around forty-six percent of CT-70s produced.

The rear of the frame no longer had a hole in the top for the taillight wire. The wire ran along the top of the frame and under the taillight bracket attaching to the taillight. The hubs no longer had circle marks on the shifter side and the opposite side of the hub and each spoke was raised in the center rather than flat. The rear brake hub arm was curved rather than flat. The rear of the muffler where the diffuser is was longer rather than stubby like the previous version. According to the Honda parts books up to serial number 118606, or the first 18,606 CT-70s, used the early style muffler that people refer to as the Silver Tag muffler. The type-two muffler supposedly started at frame number 118607 and ran up to frame number 183136.

1970 front head tube black identification tag.

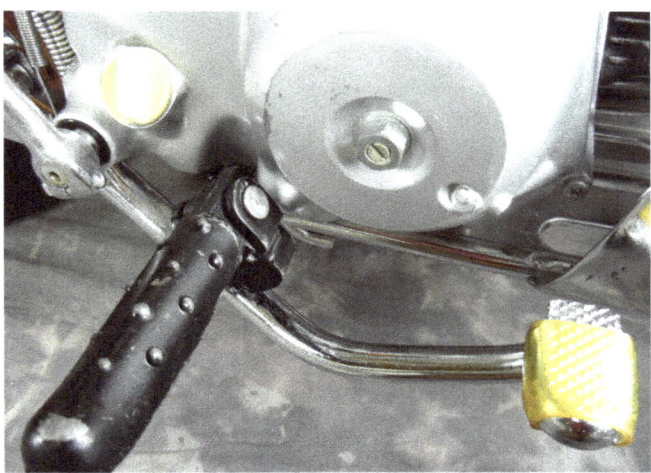

Black metal fold up foot pegs. All chrome foot pedals came with a clear rubber pad on the foot pad.

Type II black tag speedometer for the three speed model.

Bridgestone and Nitto tires were used on all black tag models.

Unique to only the first model CT-70 was the headlight that required a bulb whereas from K1 to 1982 they used a sealed beam headlight. In the speedometer, the high beam indicator was switched from fabric to an actual lens. The diamond marks were removed from the head as stated earlier and all 1970 and 1971 models had number and letter stampings. The twist knobs went from a thin Z50 looking knob to a thicker knob. The trim ring for the headlight changed to a one-piece unit. The axle had a hole in the end of it for a cotter pin and the hex nuts were switched to castle nuts because of the cotter pin. The horn eventually switched to a solid aluminum color with no black backing. Brent Kolada's Candy Gold with serial number 165913 has the early horn. The big "8" bolts were eventually switched over to bolts with a marking that looks like a pig nose or an alpha symbol. A slightly longer gas tank bracket was later added, as was the battery drain tube hole in the frame.

What overall features make the first model CT-70 unique whether Silver Tag or Black Tag? The seat cover is a one-year only design and usually considered a favorite among collectors. A black vinyl cover with a slight grain, a silver Honda name across the back, five chrome buttons along the bottom edge of the cover, and nine heat pressed

Type II brake hubs with domed center spokes on hubs

seams along the top of the cover. The plastic headlight bucket with an integrated speedometer unit is unique to the first model CT-70 as is the small taillight assembly. The entire front fork assembly with small rubber black boots and aluminum caps was unique to this model as well.

A feature the CT-70 had over the Z50 was that when you fold the handlebars down the triple clamp had an extra notch to lock the bars in place for transportation. The chrome handlebars were unique to the first model and had a close resemblance to the Z50 bars. The main body decal said "Honda" across the bar. It was white with a black outline. There was a stripe that ran vertically through the letter "N" and the stripe was black with a white pinstripe, then black, then white along the outer edge. One known variation on the three-speed first model decal is that on CTs produced in February of 1970, the black background shading is completely filled in along the bottom of the letter "A" and it is cut out on all other motorcycles produced before this month or after. Certainly a vendor variation at the time of production.

All first model CTs had chrome fenders, a chrome strip along the top of the frame, a chrome kicker, a chrome shifter, a chrome muffler, chrome

The gray T.S.K. brake cables came with integrated brake light switches front and rear.

Black rubber hand grips, black plastic hand brake levers, and black horn button mounted in the right side handlebar.

38 tooth rear sprocket on all three speed models.

Type III chain guard. Metric bolts used after Phillips head screws were phased out.

Engine serial numbers are located on the shifter side of the engine.

air cleaner caps, chrome foot brake pedal, chrome engine crash guard with spark plug guard, and a chrome taillight bracket. When the foot brake pedals left the factory, they had a clear piece of plastic on the pad to protect them. It is rare to find a CT-70 with this still on the pedal. Like the footbrake pedal, the chrome strip along the top of the frame came with a blue protective coating to protect the finish. The foot brake pedal bracket has a crude weld and a bumped out section just above where the mounting washer sits when mounted on the motorcycle. The rear shocks had aluminum tops, bottoms, and chrome coil springs. The shock covers were painted the main body color.

The battery used was a green Yuasa code 6N2A-2C. The three-position key switch was unique to the first model because of the wiring harness. An orange rectifier, as the one used on the SL-70 or Z50A, was used on the first model CT as well. According to the Honda parts manuals, all CT-70s at serial number 233054 and below used a zinc plated metal battery tray with four rubber donuts to hold the battery in place. All CT-70s at serial number 233055 required the white plastic battery tray to hold the battery in place. Because of the addition of the battery tray, a slightly longer battery strap was required. All first model CT-70s

Stanley taillight lens. Type II mufflers with extended rear outlet.

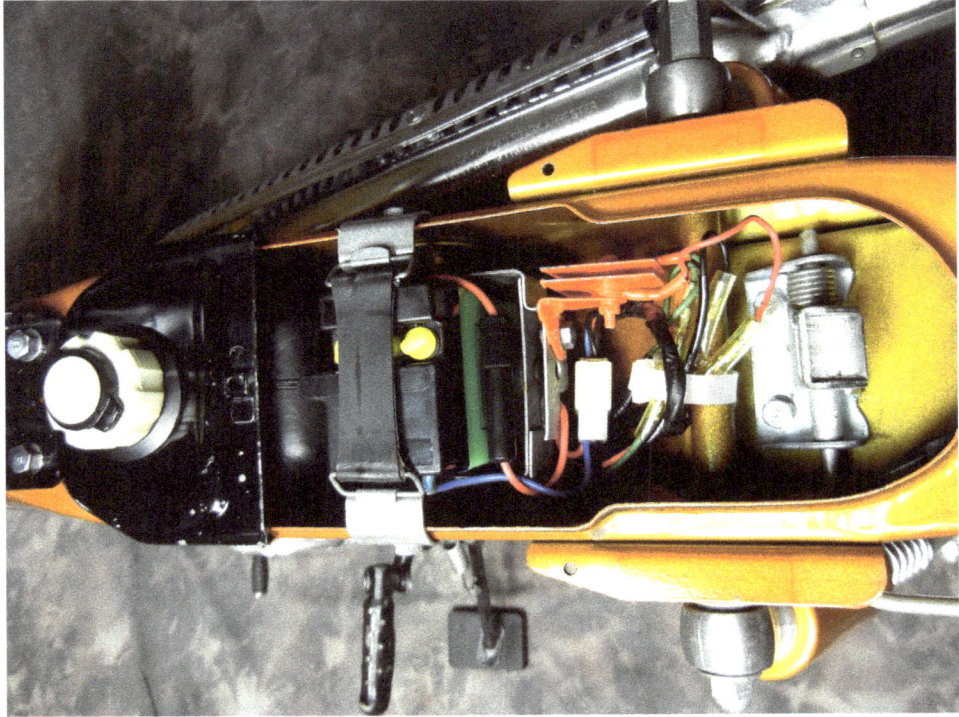

Later model frame without a taillight hole plugged with a grommet. Plastic gas tank and 6N2A-2C Yuasa battery.

NGK spark plug caps continued into the black tag run. Later replaced by "HM" stamped Honda cap.

Tall carburetor cap. Brass gas line nipples.

Candy Gold black tag. Top of frame chrome strip. Honda sticker used on all three speeds 1969-1971.

came with T.S.K. gray cables with black rubber boots. The front brake cable had a built in brake light switch and the rear did as well. The rear cable hooked into the frame and connected to the rear brake arm. The foot pegs used were black metal with fold up pegs. The pegs used 5/16 steel balls to assist in folding up. This design was exclusive to the first model CT-70 until Honda brought it back in 1991 and used it until the last 1994 CT-70 was built.

The gas tank that was used was black plastic with a white plastic cap with an on/off twist knob. Each side of the frame had metal warning decals. The kicker side badge said "Trail 70" in silver and below, "Trail 70", it gave reference to the motorcycle being manufactured for off-road use only. It also gives information about how you should not remove or modify the exhaust system. The majority of the badge was black with silver text. The badge on the shifter side said "Trail 70" on top in silver and below it, it said "Important" in red and it gave the operator instructions on how to transport the motorcycle. Like the other badge, the background was black with silver text. The rest of the features remained the same as the Silver Tag model. The highest recorded V.I.N. number I could find is serial number 285201.

A few items people ask about when restoring CT-70s are the rear racks, the rear buddy pegs, and the right side grab handle. The rear rack was not a factory Honda item, but rather a dealer installed aftermarket item. The rear buddy pegs, like the rear rack were also dealer-installed items. There are aftermarket buddy pegs as well as pegs that have the "HM" Honda logos. They have been found installed on CT-70s at the dealership but they did not come on the motorcycle from the factory. The right side frame grab handle was not installed on the U.S.A model; it only came on the DAX Model. The U.S.A model has black rubber plugs in the frame to plug the bolt-holes where the grab handle mounts.

Chapter 7

1970 H Model CT-70

Engine serial number beginning and ending: CT70H-100001
Frame number beginning and ending: CT70H-100001

In late April of 1970, Honda added a new model to their CT-70 line-up. The new model was the CT-70H. The "H" stood for hand clutch. The frames were designated H model frames evidenced by the CT-70H V.I.N. stamping. The H model came with a four-speed manual transmission and a hand clutch. With the addition of the four-speed transmission came three new color choices for six vibrant color choices for 1970. The new colors were Candy Topaz Orange, Candy Emerald Green, and Candy Teal Blue. At a glance, besides the new color choices not a lot changed between

Original unrestored Candy Teal Blue H model four speed owned by **Brent Kolada.**

43

Type II flywheel cover with removable points cover.

Nippon Seiki four-speed speedometer.

the three-speed model and the H model. The speedometer had a fourth rpm line added with a number four above it for a shifting indicator. The main body decal was completely different. The main body stripe was the same black and white pinstriped pattern; however, it was slanted at an angle. The top of the sticker said "Honda" in white and was outlined in black. Below Honda, it said "Trail 70" in red and was outlined in white.

Because of the hand clutch on the left side handlebar, the rear brake cable was eliminated. With the elimination of the rear brake cable, the foot brake pedal was the only source for rear brakes. The frame however did not eliminate the mounting peg to house the rear brake cable. A bracket was added to the carburetor to hold the clutch cable before it dropped into the top of the clutch cover. The clutch cover had a removable center cover that was held on by two Phillips head screws. With the addition of an extra gear, the rear sprocket went from thirty-eight to forty-five teeth. A fourteen-tooth front sprocket was used. The carburetor used on the H model had a different marking on it when compared to the three-speed model. CT-70s at or below serial number 150720 had a "HT7A" stamping on them. CT-70s at or above serial number 150720 had a "HT7B stamping. Brent Kolada owns a Candy Teal Blue H model with serial number 147303, built December of 1970 and it has the HT7A stamping on the carburetor. This stamping is consistent with the Honda serial number sequencing in the parts books.

All other components remained the same as the three-speed model. Production for the first model CT-70H ran until August of 1971. The highest recorded serial number I could find was CT-70H 161156. It was produced in August of 1971. A friend provided me with serial number 164047 and that particular model was produced in August of 1971 as well. I have seen V.I.N. tags

Type II large rubber twist knobs.

CT-70 H model black VIN tag. Gray T.S.K cables.

for both the first model CT-70H and the CT-70H K1 with August of 1971 production dates. Based on the highest recorded serial number, it proves that at least sixty-one thousand one-hundred and fifty-six first model H CT-70s were produced. With no actual production figures posted, based on the aforementioned serial number, it is safe to say that around sixty-two thousand were produced. A few examples of H models with colors are the following: A June of 1970 production H, with serial number 112713 came in Candy Teal Blue. A June of 1970 production H, with serial number 114495 came in Candy Emerald Green. A September of 1970 H, with serial number 131909 came in Candy Topaz Orange.

Chapter 8
CT70 1972 K1 and H K1

After 3 years with one design style, two transmission options, six color choices and thousands sold, it was time for Honda to make a change. The change was the all-new K1 model and production began in August of 1971 and ran until June of 1972. The K1 was offered in two colors choices and two transmissions. When it came to color choices, the buyer could choose between Candy Ruby Red and Candy Yellow Special. Just like the previous model, the buyer could choice between a three-speed semi-automatic transmission and a four-speed manual transmission. The K1 would be the final CT-70 that offered two transmission choices.

With every new model comes many new changes and the K1 was full of styling changes. Perhaps one of the most notable changes was the front fork. The front forks came with telescopic oil dampened shock absorbers. The fork is made up of lower legs, a steering stem, and painted upper ears to hold the headlight bucket in place. Large fork reflectors replaced the small Z50 style reflectors the previous model used. The rear of the Mini Trail had heavy-duty spring shocks with aluminum lowers, chrome coil springs, and body color shock top covers. To go along with the new front end the rear end of the motorcycle made a structural change that most people are not aware of, but it certainly was significant - the rear swing arm had extra gussets added to the inside for extra strength. This feature stayed until the end of CT70 production in 1994. The front and rear fenders were identical to the standard fenders used on the previous model and were chrome plated.

All-new handlebars were used on this model and they were more comfortable and wider apart for better control. Just like the previous model, the bars had black rubber twist knobs that could be folded down for easy storage. The bars had lever perches on each for aluminum brake levers with black rubber tips. No mirror mounts were present on the lever perches. The left side bar had a black hi/low-dimmer switch and the right side bar had a black

K1 CT-70 three-speed in Candy Ruby Red.

K1 seat with decorative chrome strip along the bottom.

black rubber gasket around the face of the unit. The speedometer had a black background with a small "HM" logo in the bottom center in white. The numbers and hash marks were white and the RPM shift point lines were green. The top left side had a green neutral light and the top right side had a red high beam indicator light.

The K1 used the same wheels and hubs as the previous model and they too were painted Cloud Silver. Bridgestone or Nitto Tires were used on the K1 model. The main body decals as well as the side metal badges were all new for the K1 as well. The main body decals on the 3-speed model were similar to the previous model with the addition of "Trail 70" below the word Honda. The stripe was light blue with white and black pin stripes and the word "Honda" was black with white outlines. "Trail 70" was yellow. The shifter side metal badge on the 3-speed was light blue on top and said "CT 70", next it said "Important" and it gave transportation information instructions for hauling in a vehicle.

Large taillight and chrome bucket with large license plate frame.

horn button. Just like the previous model year, the brake cables were gray and were T.S.K. brand. Both the front and rear cables had black rubber boots on them. The horn switch was the same as the previous model with the addition of the "TEC" logo added to the horn button. The cables and dimmer switch were secured to the bars with clear plastic cable ties. Because of the new front fork, a chrome fork bridge sat on top of the fork and an aluminum triple clamp on top of that. This type of triple clamp set up would be used until the end of production in 1978. An all-new headlight and speedometer set up was in place for 1972. Honda no longer went with a one-piece headlight and speedometer combo, but rather two separate units. The new headlight bucket was switched from plastic to metal and like the previous model used a Stanley headlight assembly and a chrome trim ring. However, this time it was a sealed beam unit unlike the previous model with a removable headlight bulb. The sealed beam headlight was used through 1982. The new speedometer was a round metal canister type with a

New two-piece triple clamp and separate speedometer and headlight bucket.

The kicker side metal badge on the 3-speed was also light blue on top and like the other badge it said "CT70" and "Important" but this time it warns against removing or modifying the exhaust system.

An all-new seat set the K1 apart from the previous model. Basic ribs across the top like most motorcycle seats were gone for the new model. This time Honda went with a box and grid pattern for the Z50A and the K1 CT-70. The most noticeable feature on the new seat was the chrome strip along the bottom edge of the seat instead of chrome buttons. A silver "Honda" logo graced the back of the seat like the previous model. The small Z50-style taillight from the previous model was replaced with a larger tail light bracket as well as an extra-large Stanley taillight lens. The kicker and shifter remained chrome like the previous model, as did the crash guard for the engine and the spark plug guard.

The ignition switch remained on the shifter side of the bike and functioned with or without lights depending on the positioning of the switch. The ignition switch looks the same as the previous model; however, it is a new switch and was used up to 1976. The wiring configuration to go with the new wire harness is what sets it apart from the previous model. The battery was also different and the Yuasa code was Y6N2A-2C-3. The handgrips remained the same as the previous model, as did the throttle assembly having no snap back return while twisting the grip. The foot peg assembly remained

Hydraulic front forks, unique to the K1 model.

K1 3-speed model main body frame decal.

K1 sales brochure with a Candy Yellow Special three speed.

almost the same as the previous model, with rounded fold up pegs with nubs. Like the previous model, they came in black. The difference between the previous models when compared to the K1 was that the previous version had ball bearings inside and the K1s had detents to hold the pegs in place.

The flywheel cover, like the majority of the previous model had a polished removable points cover that said "Honda" painted in black in the middle and "Made in Japan" on the bottom. The air cleaner visibly remained the same as the later version of the previous model with two chrome side covers and the unit black in color. New for the K1 model was an insert tray in the center of the housing for the air filter element. A large one-piece foam element helped keep the Mini Trail carburetor free of debris. The chain guard remained the same as the later version of the previous model and always came in the body color to match the rest of the bike.

The top of the chain guard, like the previous model, had a tire pressure decal in black with silver text informing the rider about the specifics of tire pressure. New for the K1 model was a helmet holder. The ignition key was used to lock and unlock the helmet holder that was mounted directly under the seat on the shifter side of the Mini Trail. A yellow sticker with black text that said "Helmet holder" was stuck to the frame just below the helmet lock. On the top of the frame, a decorative chrome strip was present to hide the welds from where the frame was fused together. This was present on all CT70s. Just in front of the seat, a sticker was placed on the frame that said, "Remember" and the warning was "Preserve Nature Always wear a helmet think safety". On the Candy Ruby Red bikes, the sticker was clear with white text and shading. If the Mini Trail was Candy Yellow Special, the sticker was clear with black text and shading. The horn remained the same as the Black Tag 1970 style horn.

Besides the front fork and the seat being major changes for the K1 model, the exhaust system was certainly a noticeable change. The complete exhaust went from chrome to a high temperature black painted unit. The two lower header pipe heat shields remained chrome like the previous model, but the large upper heat shield switched from an all chrome shield to having eight large portholes with flat black paint in the center section of the shield. The front portion of the upper heat shield had nine vertical cutouts in a row with a chrome section and then two more vertical cutouts. Honda reproduced a modern version of this heat shield. The front portion of the shield has four portholes instead of nine vertical cutouts, a chrome section, and then one final porthole. This version never came on a factory built CT-70.

The chrome footbrake pedal bracket changed to a smooth pressed together medal brake and it lacked the bump that was present on the first model bracket. However, the pedal and linkage looked and functioned the same as the previous model. Underneath the seat, besides the wiring harness, rectifier, and battery like the previous model, was the gas tank. The K1 was a transition year for parts changes. Some K1s came with left over plastic gas tanks with plastic caps and later when the plastic tanks ran out, the all-new metal gas tank with metal gas caps were used. John Milotzky of Wisconsin owns a Candy Yellow Special with a build date of October 1971 and it has a plastic gas tank and plastic gas cap. He also owns a Candy Ruby Red

*A fully restored CT-70 three speed in Candy Special Yellow owned by **John Milotzky**.*

A new wider stance handlebar and large fork reflectors set the K1 apart from the previous model.

1972 dealer advertisement for the QA 50, Z50A, and CT-70. When you purchased a new Mini Trail you received a free stocking big enough to hold a Mini Trail. The CT-70H 4 speed model with the angled main body frame decal. Final year of the H model.

model with a build date of March of 1972 and it has a metal gas tank and metal gas cap. The carburetor used on the K1 is the same as the Black Tag carburetors from the previous model. The black rubber carb cap seal has a red paint line around it; one of those details that often times is missed when doing a proper restoration or when trying to authenticate an original bike.

As mentioned earlier, an H model K1 was also available for 1972. According to the sales brochure, the "H" stands for hand clutch. Very few differences existed between the H K1 and the K1 model. The most noticeable differences were the graphics and the clutch cover on the engine. The H model was a four-speed transmission that had four gears with a downshift pattern. The right side engine cover had a removable clutch cover and a pivot arm that attached to the clutch oil cover and a hole in the top of the cover to hold the clutch cable in place. A clutch cable replaced the rear brake cable. The clutch cable was securely held in place by a bracket that was attached to an intake manifold bolt on the kicker side of the Mini Trail. The main body decal like the previous "H" had an angled stripe. The stripe was black with white and black pinstripes. The word "Honda" was written in block style writing at the top of the decal and below it, the words "Trail 70" were also in block style writing in Red outlined with a white pinstripe and black around the outer edge. The main body decals were identical for both color options. The metal badges below the seat on each side were identical to the ones used on the K1 model with the exception of the color being red instead of blue and the top line on each side read CT-70H instead of CT-70. The speedometer on the H K1 differed only slightly from the K1 model in that it had four green shift marks on the face compared to the K1 model only having three to go with the three-speed transmission.

No actual production numbers have been reported for the K1 and H K1 models. Based on recorded serial numbers, an estimated 65,000 or so K1 models and around 25,000 or so H K1 models were produced. With the production figures posted, around 90,000 units were sold in an eleven-month period, or around 8,100 or so per month.

Chapter 9
CT 70 1973 K2

Beginning serial number for all USA models-2100001

Production began around June of 1972 and ran until around May of 1973. No production numbers have been reported for this particular model. However, based on recorded serial numbers; around 45,000 or so were produced.

Nineteen seventy-three marked the beginning of the downward spiral for the CT-70 revolution. Gone were the 4-speed H models and it would not be long before color options would diminish to one and chrome would be switched to black painted parts. It was a sign of the times. Two new color options were available for nineteen-seventy three. This time you could purchase a Candy Topaz Orange model or if Blue was your

Note: The CT-70H 4 speed model with the angled main body frame decal.
Final year of the H model.

K2 Candy Riviera Blue CT-70 owned by Bill Johnson.

style, a Candy Rivera Blue model was also available. Even though Honda was slowly moving towards a simplified motorcycle, the wire harness included turn signal wires. Turn signals were not available on the K2; however, they became available the next year.

One of the biggest changes that Honda introduced for the K2 was the front fork. The upper portion of the fork went from a painted version to a chrome version. Honda did away with the oil filled front shocks and went back to coil spring shocks with large black rubber boots. Just like the previous year, the fork bridge/triple clamp remained chrome with large rubber twist knobs and

Newly designed seat with rough grain material. Chrome shock top covers. Newly designed taillight lens.

On/off switch with high/low dimmer switch.

Horn and turn signal switch. The K2 did not have turn signals. Note black knob is missing.

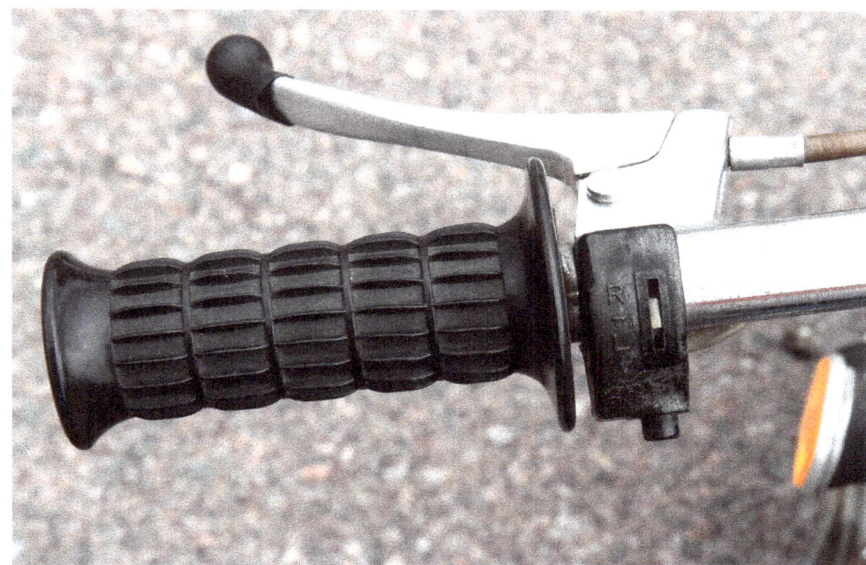

Helmet lock under the seat.

Main body decal says Honda in yellowish gold with black shadowing, outlined in white. The bottom of the decal says Trail 70 in white outlined in orange.

in white. The bottom of the decal said "Trail 70" in white outlined in orange with black shadowing outlined in white. Below the seat on each side of the frame, the frame badges were yellow with black text outlined in black with a white outer boarder. The exhaust side badge warns about modifying the exhaust system and the shifter side badge gives transporting information.

Another new change for the K2 was the foot peg assembly. The smooth solid metal foot pegs were switched to open cut out pegs with alligator teeth for increased foot grip. The pegs remained black like the previous models. The complete exhaust system introduced for the K1 model was present on the K2 model. Several items remained the same as the previous model. The wheels, rectifier, front and rear fenders, battery, foot brake pedal and brake linkage, engine crash guard, and spark plug guard. New for 1973, Honda started stamping a code into the front hubs. An example is 1-6.

chrome plated mounting bolts. The one item that did remain the same from the K1 to the K2 was the fork reflectors. The large fork reflectors that started on the K1 were present through the 1978 model year. The metal headlight bucket in black paint with a chrome headlight ring, and a Stanley headlight lens that Honda introduced the previous year, was present on this model.

Besides the new front fork, the other new feature for 1973 was the seat. The seat featured a rugged top grain with a decorative chrome strip along the bottom edge like the previous model year. Just like the front shocks, the rear shocks made a styling change as well. The rear shocks went from painted upper shock covers to chrome shock covers. The taillight bracket remained the same as the K1 including the large Stanley taillight lens. The flywheel cover made a subtle change from the K1 to the K2. The removable points cover on the K1 said "Honda" in black with the words "Made in Japan" below it. The K2 removable points cover had a black oval shaped logo in the center of the cover with the

Newly designed front fork with large fork boots, chrome uppers, and chrome fork ears

A trio of K2 CT-70s in Candy Riviera Blue and Candy Topaz orange.

word "Honda" in the center of the oval portion. The words "made in Japan" like the K1 also ran along the bottom of the points cover.

The sales brochure says "a newly styled fuel tank". The gas tank that switched from plastic to metal at the end of K1 production was the fuel tank Honda used for many years. The handlebar controls on the K2 were redesigned. Gone were the simple horn and dimmer switch. This time an on/off red safety kill switch was added and the high and low switch was incorporated into this control switch. The left side bar had a control switch with a horn button and a right and left turn signal control switch. Even though the K2 did not come with turn signals as stated earlier, the wiring harness had the wires and the left side bar control had the switch. The K2 had lever perches and mirror mounts on both handlebars. Gray front and rear T.S.K. brake cables were present on all K2 CT-70s. The speedometer at a glance appears to be identical to the previous model. The bottom of the speedometer says Nippon "Seiki" and the previous model has the "HM" logo. The indicator lights are also different from the previous model. The left side indicator light is a green neutral light and the right side indicator light is blue for high beam. A new feature for the K2 was the speedometer with shift indicator numbers on the faceplate for rpm shift points.

The main body decals were redesigned for the K2 model. The top of the decal said "Honda" in yellowish gold with black shadowing outlined

Chapter 10

CT-70 1974 K3

Beginning and ending frame serial numbers
for all USA models-2300001-2332907

Production began in May of 1973 and ran until June of 1974. Nineteen seventy-four was the last year that Honda offered two color options for the CT-70. The two color options were Candy Topaz Orange and Candy Riviera Blue. Both were the same colors as the previous model year. A bold new main body decal was used on the seventy-four.

The Top of the decal said "Honda" in black outlined in orange with a thin black pinstripe outlined with a thin white pinstripe.

The most noticeable feature of the 1974 was the addition of the front and rear turn signals. If you ever questioned whether a CT-70 was street legal, the new styling features left no question about

its purpose. The chrome front fork ears had holes to mount the chrome turn signal arms and the rear of the frame utilized the holes at the back of the frame under the seat to hold each of the chrome turn signal arms. Large round amber plastic lenses were used front and rear. Nineteen-Seventy four would be the last year Honda would use all the chrome parts on their CT-70 that were present on the previous models. It was a sign of the times and each year after, less and less chrome appeared on the motorcycle. With the addition of turn signals, a bigger battery was required. The Yuasa battery used was 6N4C-1B. This battery was present through the 1976 model year. To house the new battery, a new battery box as well as rubber liner was used. The battery box was present through the '79 production and the battery rubber insert would remain in use through 1982. The battery strap was used K3-1994. The orange rectifier used previously, was replaced with a small silicon rectifier in black made by Shindengen of Japan. This was only used on the K3 and the following year.

The rear taillight bracket, foot brake pedal, air cleaner round side covers, and spark plug guard were all chrome. This was the last year that they were available in chrome. The rear shock coils were chrome; however, 1974 would be the last year for not only the chrome upper shock covers but also the upper covers

New main body decals were used on K3 and the K4. The front fork ears added holes for the turn signal arms.

First year for the turn signals. Note the center turn signal indicator in the center of the triple clamp.

New main body decals were used on K3 and the K4. The front fork ears added holes for the turn signal arms.

in general. Front and rear fenders like the previous model years were chrome as well as the engine crash guard. The headlight bucket remained metal with gloss black paint and a chrome trim ring with a Stanley headlight unit. The taillight lens was large and was the same as the 1972 and 1973 models made by Stanley. The Aluminum CT-70 badges were present on both sides of the frame below the seat. Gone were the yellow background badges from the previous model year. The exhaust side badge warns about modifying the exhaust system and the shifter side badge gives transporting information. Both badges have a yellowish/orange border and the words CT-70 on top. The exhaust system that Honda introduced in 1972 with the two chrome lower heat shields and the one-piece chrome upper heat shield with large round portholes and flat black paint was present on the 1974 model.

When Honda introduced the rough grain seat in 1973, it was a seat design that was used for several model years. The seat, like those used the previous two years, had the decorative chrome strip along the bottom edge and tool kit compartment on the bottom of the seat pan. The brake plates, hubs, and rim dishes remained the same as the previous model years and were painted Cloud Silver. The right side handle bar switch was black with a red on/off twist knob for the safety kill switch. It also featured a hi/lo dimmer slide that was integrated into the switch as well. The left side switch also

Candy Riviera Blue paint with metal warning badges under the seat outlined in yellow and black.

came in black and had a turn signal slide and the horn button. This was the last year that these two handle bar controls were present on a CT-70. The handlebars featured lever perches for front and rear hand brakes on each bar on the early models. Later in the production run, the left brake lever was eliminated, and all that remained was a small mirror perch.

This was the last year that Honda would use two lever perches and hand brake levers on the CT-70. When the left hand brake lever was removed, so was the rear brake cable. This also prompted the addition of a front brake light switch to be added to the right side lever perch. A different foot brake pedal was used on the early models, and switched when the bars and elimination of the rear brake pedal took place. The early foot brake pedal required the brake pedal middle arm and the rear brake wire arm. The later bikes required a new foot brake pedal that had an arm added to it so it could pull the rear brake rod since the two mechanisms were not required. With the elimination of the rear brake cable the front brake panel added, wear indicators. The indicators were most likely added to gage the amount of wear the front brakes had due to the loss of the rear brake cable. The parts guides reference all bikes at or below serial number 2320001 requiring the early parts and all bikes at serial number 2320002 requiring the later parts because of the removal of the rear brake cable. Here are a few examples of production bikes with serial numbers to show the parts changes.

Serial number 2306904 with a build date of September 1973 has a brake switch in the front brake cable; it has a rear brake cable, two lever perches with mirror mounts, and the early foot brake pedal that requires the two mechanism pieces to pull the rear brake rod. Serial number 2327613 with a build date of April 1974 has a mirror mount only on the left bar, no brake lever mount on the left bar, a perch mounted brake switch on the right bar, and no rear brake cable. Based on the available production numbers and serial number ranges for the parts changes, the final 12,905 CT70s had the new bars, foot pedal, and lacked the rear brake cable. With the elimination of the rear brake cable, it eliminated the cable guide on the air box housing. The foot pegs like the previous year, had the springs in the pegs to fold up easily if they hit a solid object while riding. The kickstand did not come with a rubber pad like the following model year, however it is not out of the question for a rubber-padded kickstand to be present on an end of model year motorcycle. The 1974 K3 was the last CT70 with a downshift transmission. The twist knob of the carburetor from 1974 back takes a ¼ turn to shut it off. The lever is on the right side of the carburetor.

By year's end, production topped out at 32,907 CT70 Mini Trail motorcycles.

The rough grain seat used on the K2 model was also used on the K3 model. The rear turn signals mounted in the holes in the rear of the frame.

Chrome rear shock top covers, a carryover from the previous model.

Gray T.S.K. brake cables with black rubber boots were used on the front of all K3s. Note: not all K3 models had a rear brake cable, as it was a mid-year model production change

Chapter 11
CT-70 1975 K4

Beginning and ending frame serial
number for all USA models-2400001-2408852
Carburetor Serial Number 533A

Production began in June of 1974. The K4 that I got when I was 12 years old is the 5,443rd produced. It has a build date of 10/74. Based on these production figures the K4 production would have finished production by the very beginning of 1975 or so.

Nineteen-seventy five was a significant year for the Honda CT-70. It was the first time in CT-70 history that Honda went with one color option. Similar to the early 1970's Chrysler Cuda Sublime Green, Honda had their own version and Mighty Green was the color. The one color choice was a sign of the times for not only Honda CT-70 production, but for the Z50A as well. To go with

An all original low mile Mighty Green K4 1975 Honda CT-70 owned by Brent Kolada.

The main body decals remained the same as the previous model year. Only one frame color was offered for the K4 model.

the single color option came a number of style changes that appeared to be cost-saving measures rather than styling changes. The Spark plug guard, tail light bracket, triple clamp, round air box side covers, and foot brake pedal all switched from a shiny chrome finish to black painted components. The sales brochure for nineteen-seventy five explains the new look as such, "The look of this popular little bike is more stylish than ever! With just the right amount of chrome, color and flat black paint treatments to make it a hit." Once the chrome parts go away, they usually do not come back and this was certainly the case for the CT-70.

Nineteen-seventy five was the last year that Honda used a gray speedometer cable and throttle cable. To match the cables, the bar controls were also outfitted with gray sheathing as well. One thing to keep in mind when restoring your Mighty Green CT-70 is to be cognizant that most service replacement control switches that you will find for this particular model will come with black sheathing rather than gray sheathing. If you want your K4/seventy-five to look like it did when it left the factory, you will want gray sheathing on your switches.

The speedometer changed for nineteen-seventy five as well.

Honda did away with the small hash marks in the speedometer, which indicated a mile per hour for each hash mark. The new speedometer had a medium sized white mark for each five-mile per hour increment and a large bold white line for every ten miles per hour. It also included neutral and high beam indicator lamps in the speedometer.

Nineteen seventy-five was definitely a transition year. One particular part that certainly was a transition part was the rear turn signal mounting bar. On my particular early production K4, it has chrome turn signal mounting arms front and rear. As production went on Honda changed the turn signal arms to a black mounting arm in the rear and they kept the chrome mounting arms on the front of the motorcycle. Brent Kolada owns a later production Mighty Green with black rear turn signal mounting arms and chrome front mounting arms.

By nineteen-seventy-five, dual hand brakes were eliminated, most likely to cut costs. The K4 was the first full model to feature one hand brake lever. It was a right hand mounted front brake lever integrated into the right hand on/off kill switch assembly. Gone were the small aluminum hand brake levers. This time Honda went with a large motocross style lever with a clear protective coating and a black rubber tip. The right hand kill

Black rear turn signal mounting arms are present on this particular Mini Trail and some left the factory with left over chrome arms

The hash marks were eliminated from the speedometer face. K4 was the last model to use all gray cables. Front turn signal arms came in chrome on all K4s.

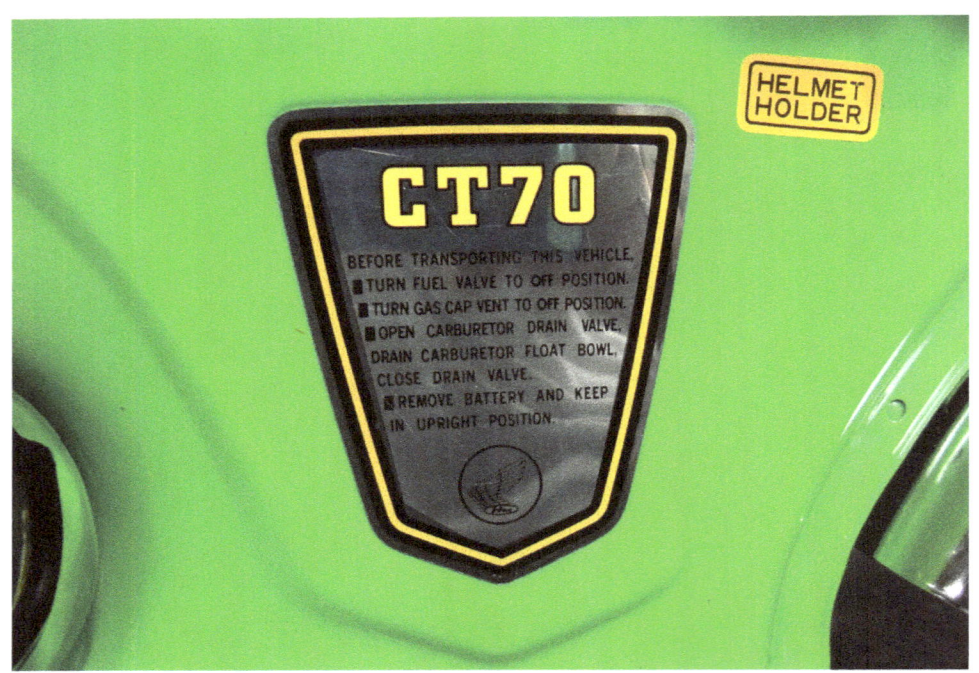

The transportation badges were metal with black and yellow graphics. A helmet holder sticker was applied to all K4 frames just below the seat.

switch assembly also hand a mirror mount integrated into it since the bars made a change as well. The bar assembly was changed for seventy-five to a style that lacked lever perches like the previous model year. The left side bar came with a control switch in black to match the right hand side switch. The left switch had the turn signal switch up top, the horn button in the middle, and the hi/lo switch at the bottom of the assembly. The text on each switch came highlighted in red for easy visibility.

The main body decal for each side of the frame said "Honda" in black outlined in yellow with a bit of white around the

Rear shock top covers were eliminated for the K4 model.

outer edges with bold aggressive "1970's" style font. Below the word Honda, it said "Trail70" in bright blue outlined in black with a bit of white around the outer edges like the upper portion of the one-piece decal. Each side of the frame had "CT70" metal badges below the seat. The Aluminum CT-70 badges were present on both sides of the frame below the seat. The exhaust side badge warns about modifying the exhaust system and the shifter side badge gives transporting information. Both badges have a yellowish/orange border and the words CT70 on top.

Nineteen-seventy five was the last year Honda went with a rugged grain seat cover with ribs on the top and a decorative chrome strip along the bottom edge. This seat design was present on all 1973-1975 models. Like the previous models, this style had a tool kit compartment on the bottom center of the seat with a metal tool kit clip.

The rear shocks on the K4 were aluminum on the top and bottom with chrome coil springs. The

The tail light bracket came in black paint on the K4 model.

chrome top caps were no longer present on this model year. The wheels and hubs like the previous model year were painted cloud silver with polished aluminum brake plates. The kickstand underwent a change for '75 and Honda added a black rubber stabilizer pad to the side of the kickstand. The black stabilizer pad was present from K4-1982. Just like the previous model, the 6N4C-1B Yuasa battery, battery box, and battery rubber insert were present. The K4 marked the first year for the three-speed up shift pattern transmission. A pattern that would continue for the rest of the life of the CT-70. The carburetor petcock made a change, it went from a ¼ turn shutoff to a ½ turn shutoff and the lever was on the left side of the carburetor.

By years end, 8,852 Mighty Green CT-70 Mini Trails were produced.

K4 was the last model CT-70 to use this particular type of V.I.N. tag.

67

Chapter 12

CT-70 1976 Honda

Beginning and ending frame serial numbers for all USA models-2500004~2505533
Beginning engine serial number for all USA models-2500001
Carburetor serial number-533 A

Like all models, due to U.S.A federal regulations, manufacturers were required to declare model year designations and the "K" model name was dropped. All 1976 models and beyond were referred to by the year and no longer a model name. Orange was a color that Honda introduced in 1970 when the 4-speed H model hit the showroom floors and a variation of the color was back again for 1976 as well as other years. The '76 model came in Tahitian Red. The 1976 model year ushered in new changes while keeping some of the features from the previous model years.

The main body decals said "Trail 70" in

Yellow, outlined in White, with a black background. The Word "Honda" appeared below in Blue, outlined in White, with a black background. Three yellow hash marks with a black border accompanied the main body decal. 1976 was the final year for the tough grain ribbed seat. The center of the seat had heat pressed seams. The seat had piping around the upper edge and a decorative chrome strip along the bottom edge. The word "Honda" was on the back of the seat in a silver/grayish tone vinyl paint. The seat had a black seat pan with a spot welded tool kit compartment with a zinc coated wire clip in the top center like the previous model year.

Instead of chrome on the upper section of the front forks like the previous model, the upper portion was painted Tahitian Red to match the frame, rear swing arm, and chain guard. The large aggressive black rubber fork boots that Honda introduced in 1973 were present on the '76 model.

The front and rear fenders came in chrome and they were the same fenders used on the previous model year. Like the previous years, again with the exception of the Silver-Tag hubs, the wheels, hubs, and brake

1976 Tahitian Red CT-70 owned by Bill Johnson.

All new black triple clamp and black cables for 1976.

Tough grain pattern seat with heat pressed seams. Used 1973-1976.

The only model to have the main body decal with the words "Trail 70" on top.

Rear shocks without shock top covers. Black taillight bracket and chrome turn signal arms.

plates were the same as the previous models in that the wheels came in Cloud Silver with clear-coated polished aluminum brake plates. A carryover from the 1975 K4 were the turn signal assemblies. They too came with black mounting arms in the rear and chrome in the front. Chrome bases housed the round amber lenses. The taillight bracket was also a carryover from the 1975 model in that it was black with a large red Stanley lens with a chrome base. The top of the taillight bracket had a white with black text battery caution decal.

The throttle cable, front brake cable, and control switch casings were black on the '76 model. Just like the previous year, only one hand brake lever came on the motorcycle and it was a large motocross style with a black rubber tip and a clear protective coating. The handlebar controls were the same as the previous model year. The

Black turn signal arms, black taillight bracket with license plate frame, and large Stanley taillight lens.

left side control had the turn signal switch, a horn, and a hi/low beam switch. The right side switch was the on/off kill switch, a safety feature that became a mainstay since its inception in 1973 with the K2 model. Both bar mounted control switches had threaded mirror mounts, a feature that started with the previous model year. The rear shocks without the upper shock covers, the engine cradle spark plug guard, and the triple clamp in black were carry-over items from the previous model year. The large rubber fork boots and the aggressive foot pegs were also a carryover from the previous model year.

The flat black muffler system that came out in 1972 was also used on the 1976. It also featured the same upper heat shield in chrome with large portholes and flat black paint in the center section. Two chrome lower heat shields were used on the header pipe like the previous models. 1976 models would be the last to use

The foot brake pedal, spark plug guard, foot peg assembly, and kickstand all came in black.

1976 was the last model to use the upper muffler mounting spacer to mount the muffler.

the muffler spacer to mount the muffler. The black handgrips with a ribbed pattern were a carryover from the previous model year. A turn signal indicator was mounted in the center of the triple clamp that flashed when the turn signals were in use. This along with a flasher mounted under the seat started with the 1974 model. The speedometer that came on the '76 was the same as the previous model year. The speedometer did not have individual hash marks for each mile per hour. The speedometer went up to fifty miles per hour like the ones used on the 1972-1974 models, and had large markers for each ten-mile per hour speed like the previous model year. 1976 models were the last CT-70 to have a chrome metal upper main body frame molding until it was added back into the parts line-up in 1991. Just like the previous model, the 6N4C-1B Yuasa battery and battery box were used. This was the final year for this particular battery and battery box.

According to CT-70 guru Gary Lewis, the 1976 model is one of the hardest models to not only find in low hour original condition, but to find in any condition. If you own a 1976, consider yourself lucky. Only 5,529 Tahitian Red CT-70 Mini Trails were produced in 1976.

Chapter 13

CT-70 1977 Honda

Beginning and ending frame serial numbers for all USA models-2600008-2611967
Beginning engine serial number for all USA models-2600001
Carburetor serial number-533 A

Nineteen-Seventy Seven had many features that were present on early model CT-70s as well as some of the modern features that were a year or so away from being phased out. The 1977 model came in "Shiny Orange" paint with a mix of chrome and black painted parts. The carburetor used on the '77 was the final time it would be found on a CT-70. This particular carburetor was used 1974-1977. Several parts found on the '77 model were used on other models and they are the following parts: the wide taillight lens (used K3-'79), the turn signals in chrome (K3-'79), the tail light bracket in black (K4-'79), black spark plug guard (K4-'78), seat with a

1977 "Shiny Orange" CT-70 with all new box and grid pattern seat. First year for single position key switch.

Rear buddy peg holes welded up on the rear swing arm. Newly designed upper muffler bracket. Last year of the chrome rear shock coils.

rectangular box and grid heat pressed pattern on the top center of the seat with a decorative chrome strip along the bottom ('76-'78), engine cradle in chrome with rounded spark plug mounting tabs (late K0-'78), black ribbed handle grips (K4-'78), fork bridge in semi-glazed black (K4-'78), black foot brake pedal ('77-'79), step bar and kickstand with rubber pad (K4-'79), black metal headlight bucket and headlight assembly (K1-'79), a black muffler with large upper heat shield with large port-holes in the chrome with flat black paint in the center panel (K1-'78).

The difference in the '77 muffler compared to the previous model was that it did not require a metal spacer to get the top bracket away from the seat. This time Honda put an extra bend in the top muffler bracket to get it away from the seat and the frame. This style muffler was present up to 1982. Additional sharing of parts with models from other years include: Chrome rear shock coils (K4-'77), a round canister black air cleaner assembly (K1-'78), black right and left handle bar control switches (K4-'79), cloud silver wheels and hubs (K0-'82), front and rear brake panels ('77-'78), front fork tubes/boots/ (K1-'79), the painted fork covers were unique to each particular model because of the colors, however they were interchangeable.

The '77 was the first CT-70 to go without rear buddy peg mounting holes in the rear swing arm. This was a sign of the times as more and more safety features were added each year. The rear swing arm was modeled after the first run swing arm, as the holes were tack welded up at the factory before paint was applied. The main body decal used on the '77 is unique to this particular model. It featured the words "Trail 70" on top in white outlined in black, with the word "Honda" below it in blue outlined in white with black background fill. Three yellow stripes with black boarders also accented the main body of the CT-70. Aluminum CT-70 badges were present on both sides of the frame below the seat. The top of the frame molding on the main body of the CT-70 switched from chrome metal to a chrome plastic piece. The exhaust side badge warns about modifying the exhaust system and the shifter side badge gives transporting information. Both badges have a yellowish/orange border and the words CT70 on top. The badges were present on all 1974-1979 models.

The speedometer used on the 1977 model was a one-year exclusive speedometer. The handlebars on the 1977 model were the same

Ribbed grips used K4-1978, black control switch with turn signal knob, horn, and hi/low switch

Black on/off kill switch with mirror and brake lever mount.

Black triple clamp used K4-1978, black cables, and chrome front turn signal arm. One year only speedometer.

All new front fork. The uppers and the headlight mounting brackets were painted to match the main body color. A new horn and mount was added to the fork as well.

as the late 1975 K4 and the 1976 K5 bars. The bars featured dual mirror mounts and like the 1975-1976 models, a large motocross style brake lever with a clear protective coating and a black rubber tip was present on the 1975-1979 models. The black rubber handgrips with raised ribs were present on the '77 model as well as all 1975-1978 models. Nineteen-seventy-seven was the first year for the single position key switch. When the ignition switch is in the on position, the lights remain on. New for '77 was the horn mount bracket mounted to the backside of the shifter side fork leg. A new horn was present as well. This time a horn with eight holes around the outside and one in the center was the new design. This style horn was used for another six years. In 1977 Honda switched from round-headed axles to hex heads. This design change would last until the end of production in 1994. The plastic steering dust cover cap under the triple clamp switched from gray to black in '77.

By years end, 11,959 1977 Shiny Orange CT70 Mini Trails were produced.

72cc engine with removable points cover. The transmission featured a 3-speed up-shift pattern.

Chapter 14
CT-70 1978 Honda

Beginning and ending frame serial numbers for all USA models-2700005-2706886
Beginning engine serial number for all USA models-2700001
Carburetor serial number-PB36A A

The 1978 model CT-70 would have some firsts and certainly many lasts in terms of styling features. For the first and only time in Honda CT-70 history Honda went with a black frame, fork, and swing arm. The gloss black paint went well with many of the already blacked out parts.

The following parts featured low shine black paint: the shifter, spark plug guard, tail light bracket, shock coils, foot brake pedal, complete air cleaner assembly, and foot peg assembly. The foot peg assembly and the foot brake pedal in black were used on all 1977-1979 CT-70s. The stand rubber that mounts to the bottom of the kickstand was present on this model and was used on the

1978 CT-70, the only CT-70 to come in black. The correct seat for this particular model is the box and grid pattern seat pictured below.

Correct seat for all 1977-1978 model CT-70s.

1975-1979 models. The black spark guard was used on all 1975-1978 models. Nineteen-seventy-eight would be the first year that Honda used black shock coils and this design would last until the end of production in 1994. Chrome was not completely eliminated quite yet, thus giving the '78 a nice balance between chrome and black paint. Nineteen-seventy eight would be the last model to feature a chrome upper exhaust heat shield, fold down handlebars, and chrome fenders. It was also the last model to feature the engine cradle crash bar assembly, an item many considered a must have for trail riding. The headlight ring and turn signal mounting arms were also chrome. The headlight ring would remain chrome until the last CT-70 rolled off the assembly line in 1994. The 1978 model would be the second to last model to feature the separate headlight and speedometer combination, a feature that started with the 1972 K1 model. 1980-1981 would feature a different combination of the separate headlight and speedometer assembly. It would also be the second to last model to have a left side mounted ignition switch assembly until it came back in 1991. The handlebars had mirror mounts on each bar. Both bars had black control switches with black cables as well. The left side bar had a switch that controlled the turn signals, the horn, and the hi and low beam lights. The right side bar had a red on/off switch.

The use-what-you-have theory often times works well in production work and this was certainly the case for the 1978 CT-70. The seat used on the '78 was the same seat as the 1976 and 1977 models. What is interesting about the seat is that it was called a double seat in the parts books; however, there are no rear buddy peg holes in the rear swing arm. As safety features were popping up left and right it was an unusual situation but likely because it was a transition model. The seat had a vinyl cover with a heat pressed box and grid pattern in the top center of the seat with piping around the top edge and a decorative chrome strip along the bottom edge. The back of the seat featured a large bold "Honda" logo in white. 1978 would be the last CT-70 to come with a left side helmet lock assembly until it was brought back for the 1991 model year. This particular helmet locking assembly was used on all 1972 K1-1978 models.

Lighting features on the 1978 model include large front fork reflectors, a large visible tail light lens, and a large headlight lens. The frame decal on the '78 featured the words "Mini-Trail 70" in an orange/yellowish color outlined in white with the word "Honda below it also in white. Three stripes accented the main body as well in red/orange/yellow. Aluminum CT-70 badges were present on both sides of the frame below the seat.

Last year of the fold down handlebars.

Last year for the chrome upper muffler heat shield with flat black port holes.

Last year for the engine cradle protector. Some 1978s came without verbiage on the clutch cover.

Last year for the ribbed grips. Used K4-1978. Large aluminum brake lever with rubber tip and clear protective coating used K4-1978.

Final CT-70 with chrome fenders.

The exhaust side badge warns about modifying the exhaust system and the shifter side badge gives transporting information. Both badges have a yellowish/orange border and the words CT70 on top. The frame badges were used on all '77-'79 models. A Championship white decal was present on the top of the frame in front of the seat that read, "Remember - Preserve Nature - always wear a helmet." The 1978 model featured a brand new carb design, it would be one of several times Honda would switch carburetors during the production of the CT70. This time the carburetor had a round bottom bowl and a black plastic choke lever. The round bowl design would carry on until the last CT70 rolled off the assembly line in 1994. The unique feature about this particular carburetor is that it is the only CT70 carburetor with the petcock valve at the rear of the carburetor.

Nineteen-seventy-eight marked the first year that Honda went without verbiage on the right side clutch/crank case oil cover, however it was a cross over model year where some bikes had verbiage and some did not. The air cleaner assembly for the '78 featured black round side covers like the 1975-1977 models. The air cleaner assembly for the '78 was a one-year only assembly. Nineteen-seventy-eight would be the last year with this style air cleaner

Large Yuasa battery and turn signal flasher mounted under the seat to power the turn signals. Metal fuel tank.

before Honda added a breather tube to the air cleaner housing. The front and rear brake panels were present on this model as well as the 1977. The 1978 model would be the last time Honda used the fold down handle bar set up. This was a sign of the times as Honda was moving towards the BMX/motocross style look for its future models. The speedometer used on the 1978 model with a 50mph and 80 Km/h face as well as a neutral and high beam indicator light was new for the 1978 model year and were used 1978-1979. In '78, Honda started stamping the rims with a "DOT" marking and then Honda put the exact date the rim was produced. An example is the following: the 8,388th bike produced has 7-14-1977 stamped in the rim dish.

By years end, 6,881 Black 1978 Honda CT-70 Mini Trail motorcycles were produced.

The only CT-70 Honda ever painted black

No buddy peg mounts are present on the 1978 model. They were eliminated in 1977.

Chapter 15

CT-70 1979 Honda

Beginning frame serial number for all USA models-5000021
Beginning engine serial number for all USA models-5000021
Carburetor serial number-PB37A D

For the first time and only time in Honda history, yellow was used as the Primary frame color on a CT-70. The Honda name for the paint color was "Bright Yellow" for 1979. Several new features were ushered in for the new model year. Many of these changes would be the standard for the remaining CT-70s produced. The most noticeable changes were the absence of the engine crash guard and the fold-down handlebars. The crash bar holes were plugged with black rubber plugs from the factory. The '79 also lacked the helmet holder and the frame was plugged with two black rubber plugs. Nineteen-seventy-nine saw new model changes for both the Z50A and

the CT70. Both came with new black high-rise handlebars with risers that resembled BMX style bars. This was the direction Honda was heading for the remainder of the Mini Trail production.

One common denominator between the Z50R and the CT-70 for 1979 was the lack of chrome parts. A one-year-only black triple clamp complimented the black handlebars, footbrake pedal, taillight bracket, headlight bucket, air box, foot pegs, cables, and shifter. All new, for 1979 was a solid black upper muffler guard and rear turn signal mounting arms. Nineteen-seventy-nine, like the 1975-1978, featured black rear turn signal mounting arms. The lower header pipe heat shield and front turn signal mounting arms remained chrome for '79. The kick-starter arm for whatever reason remained chrome rather than black like the majority of the components. All-new for 1979 was a rough grained seat cover. It lacked a top design pattern or heat pressed seems like previous models. The seat did have the piping like the previous models and the Honda logo in the rear as well as the decorative chrome strip along the bottom of the seat. A tool kit compartment was present as well.

Just like the main body paint being a one-year-only color, the fenders for the

The first model to come without an engine cradle. Note: See the previous page, it could be added. All new black shock coils without shock top covers.

Handle bar risers were added to accommodate the newly designed handlebars. No rubber trim ring was present on the 1979 newly designed speedometer.

Rims were date coded on this particular model as well as some of the previous years.

A newly designed seat was introduced in 1979. The seat top was completely smooth and a chrome strip was present along the bottom.

The taillight remained the same as the previous model. Turn signal arms were black

first time ever in CT-70 history were "painted" metal and they too were yellow. The main body decals for 1979 were red/orange/yellow hash marks in the background with the words "Mini-Trail 70" in yellow with a black background and the word "Honda" below it in white. The speedo came with a decal that read, "Warning break-in maintenance required at 600 miles" and the top bar on the shifter side of the bike had a decal that said, "Remember-preserve nature-always wear a helmet - think safety." Nineteen-seventy-nine would be the last year to use the separate speedometer unit not integrated into the headlight bucket. The '79 speedometer lacked the rubber trim ring around the outer edge of the speedometer to protect the edges. The aluminum frame badges were the same as the previous model year and as mentioned earlier, were used 1974-1979. Several parts remained the same as the previous model year.

Nineteen-seventy-nine was the last year of the side mounted ignition switch in the frame until Honda brought it back in 1991. The front fork leg reflectors had black plastic around the edges instead of aluminum like all of the previous models. A new grip design came out for the '79 and it would be used on the remaining CT-70s as well as all 1979-1999 Z50Rs. The new grip was a box and grid pattern black rubber type with round donuts on the ends. The handle bar controls were the same black controls used on previous models. The right side lever mount on/off switch and the left side turn signal/horn/light switch was used on all K4-79 models.

Turn signals were present on the 1979 and they once again remained round with a chrome finish and amber lenses. The turn signal design used on the '79 was used on all K3-'79 models. The large visible tail light lens was used on all K3-'82 models. The tail light base on the '79 has been found in chrome, a left over part from the previous model year as well as the new version, which is black plastic. The sales brochure shows the black plastic version. Nineteen-seventy-nine was the first year to have a mounting tab attached to the kicker side of the swing arm to hold the engine oil overflow drain tube. This concept would carry on until the end of production in 1994. New for 1979 was the air cleaner assembly, with a rubber air breather tube that ran out the top side of the air cleaner canister and through a hole in the frame on the kicker side of the Mini Trail. Just like the previous year, a silver caution label was applied to the top of the air cleaner with black text. The rear shocks on the '79 had nineteen coils painted black and the bottoms were aluminum. Nineteen-seventy-nine was the first CT-70 that lacked verbiage on the clutch cover from the start of production to the end of production. The bolt in the frame just above the two chain guard mounting bolts is new for '79. It is to remove the coil bracket inside the frame. A feature unique to only the 1979 CT70 is the bracket that mounts between the bottom two-handle bar risers and holds the blinker light for the turn signals.

Production numbers have been reported at 7,500 for the 1979 model year. Jesse Kimball of Grand Marais Minnesota owns serial number 7,941.

All new painted fenders for 1979 in "Bright Yellow" to match the frame. Tall BMX style bars were introduced in 1979.

Last year for the frame mounted ignition switch.

All new fully black painted upper exhaust heat shield.

Black plugs present to fill in the helmet lock holes.

Frame serial number location on all CT-70 models.

Factory owner's manual.

Factory dealer sales brochure.

Plastic chrome strip on top the frame.
One year only frame decals.

Chapter 16
CT-70 1980 Honda

Beginning serial number for all USA models-5100001

The 1980 CT-70 took on a whole new look. The new design was part of a three year run for the USA model. Just like the previous year, one color was available for 1980, Tahitian Red. The main body decal said "Honda" and it had a stripe that was red, orange, and yellow. The stripes came in black with a white outer border. On the shifter side of the frame just below the seat was a black with white text emissions control warning label. On each side of the frame on the outside of the fuel tank, there were also two stickers. The shifter side sticker said "Mini Trail 70," on the kicker side the sticker was an exhaust warning with tire pressure and vehicle capacity information. The right side sticker was clear

First year without a frame mounted ignition switch. Tahitian Red 1980 - Owned by Bill Johnson.

First CT-70 to have a dash cluster to house the ignition switch and speedometer.

with black text. The left side sticker colors matched the main body decal.

The front fender came in Tahitian red and it was made of plastic. This was a longer dirt bike style type of fender compared to the painted version of the original style fender that was present on the previous model year. The cable guide moved from the front fender to the front fork right below the fender for '80. It remained in this location through 1982. New for 1980 was a redesigned front fork. The Showa Company made the front fork for Honda. The new fork was present on all 1980-1982 models as well as all 1991-1994 models. The fork tubes went from a large tube style to skinny metal tubes with black fork reflector brackets and black metal headlight ears with holes for mounting the headlight and turn signal arms. Because of the new smaller fork tubes, a new fork bridge/triple clamp was used on this model. The fork had sweeper-style seals and internal springs. The rear shocks had chrome lowers with black coil springs and aluminum uppers. Unlike the nineteen coils in 1979, 1980 switched to sixteen coils. The complete exhaust system was black with a black upper shield and this time Honda went with two lower black heat shields. The muffler was present on all 1977-1982 CT-70s.

The rear fender, like the previous year, came in metal and was painted Tahitian Red to match the frame color. The wheels and hubs were cloud silver metallic like the previous model year. The biggest change from 1979 to 1980 was the addition of a center dash assembly like those used on full size motorcycles. The dash assembly housed the ignition switch in the bottom right side corner. Above the ignition switch was an amber turn signal indicator light and to the right of it was a green neutral light. All new for 1980, the indicator lights were moved to the top right side of the dash assembly from the speedometer. The speedometer made up the entire left side of the dash assembly. The speedometer was redesigned for 1980 switching from green and white to red and white numbers on a black background. Honda plugged the hole in the frame with a black rubber plug where the ignition was mounted on the previous models. A redesigned headlight bucket was used on this model. This time the high beam indicator in blue was mounted on the top center of the black metal headlight bucket. The headlight bucket was used from 1980-1982. The headlight unit itself was used K1-1982.

The handlebar assembly remained the same BMX-style bar with two-piece aluminum risers

Tahitian Red plastic front fender, new squared off turn signals, a center mounted horn, and BMX style handle bars.

A solid black muffler system, black taillight bracket, and solid black air cleaner assembly.

1980 V.I.N. tag with model year printed on it per U.S.A regulations set forth in 1976.

held together with two mounting bolts. However, the handlebar was new for 1980 and was used on the 1981 and 1982 CT-70s as well. The handlebar controls were switched from black to aluminum for 1980. The right side switch was an on/off red twist knob kill switch assembly. The left side switch incorporated the turn signal left and right side switch, the hi/lo headlight switch, and the yellow horn button. The switches were used on all 1980-1982 CT-70s. The hand brake lever mounted on the right side of the bike came in aluminum without a black rubber tip. The front brake cable as well as the throttle cable came in black like the previous model year. A new feature for 1980 was the addition of a black rubber lever cover that covered the lever where it mounts in the control switch. The lever cover was used until the last CT-70 rolled off the assembly line in 1994.

A redesigned carburetor was introduced in 1980 and it would be a two-year carburetor, used from 1980-1981. The tail light bracket was black and was used from 1976-1982. It used the same tail light lens as all 1972-1982 model CT-70s. The air cleaner assembly was a carryover design from 1979 with a rubber air breather tube that ran out the topside of the air cleaner canister and through a hole in the frame on the kicker side of the Mini Trail.

A new rough grain seat was introduced in 1980.

Just like the previous year, a silver caution label was applied to the top of the air cleaner with black text. The black foot brake pedal was used on all 1980-1982 CT-70s.

The turn signals were a one-year set up along with the mirrors. The mirrors had chrome stems and mirror backings. The box and grid pattern grips that were introduced in 1979 were also used on the 1980 model. The grips were used on all 1979 to 1982 CT-70s as well as all 1991-1994 CT-70s. New for 1980 was a black metal lower chain guide that mounts to the rear swing arm. An all-new seat was issued in 1980 and it would be used on the 1981 and 1982 models as well. The new seat was black vinyl with a slight grain to it with angled piping on each side and a large bright white Honda logo stenciled on the rear of the seat. The bottom of the seat was black-painted metal with a storage compartment and a tool kit holder. Under the seat in the frame was the gas tank, battery, turn signal flasher, wire harness, and rectifier. The battery used was a 6N4-2A-6 Yuasa battery.

The horn used on this model was made of metal with eight holes around the outside edges and one in the center. This style horn was used on all 1977-1982 CT-70s. The kicker and shifter came in black. The top head cover switched in 1980 from 8 vertical lines to a cross pattern of four vertical lines top and bottom and three finned cooling fins on each side. The foot peg assembly, including the kickstand, is a one-year-only set up. The angle and the welding differs from that of 1981-1982. This change made the kickstand one inch shorter than the next two years. New for 1980 and used through 1982 was the gas cap. It had six high spots and six indented spots around the outside edges for easy twisting and two small vent holes in the top of the cap for ventilation. The gas cap like the tank was metal.

By 1980 year's end a total of 8,599 CT-70s were produced.

Plastic chain guard in Tahitian Red.

Showa skinny forks with black fork caps, black cables, and Cloud Silver rims and hubs.

Box and grid pattern grip, aluminum brake lever, aluminum on/off kill switch, and new black rubber brake lever cover.

Chapter 17
CT-70 1981 Honda

Beginning serial number for all USA models-JH2DD0101BS200002

The 1981 CT-70 was more or less a continuation of the previous model year with a few subtle changes. The new design was part of a three year run for the USA model. Just like the previous year, the 1981 model came in Tahitian Red. The main body decal said "Honda" in black outlined in white and it had a stripe that was white, blue, and black. The stripes were outlined in black with a white outer boarder. On the shifter side of the frame, just below the seat was a black with white text emissions control warning label. On each side of the frame, on the outside of the fuel tank there were two additional stickers. The shifter side sticker said "Mini Trail 70" and the kicker

side sticker had an exhaust warning with tire pressure and vehicle capacity information. The right side sticker was clear with black text. The left side sticker colors matched the main body decal. The front fender came in Tahitian Red and it was made of plastic. This fender was a longer dirt bike style fender compared to the painted original style fender.

New for 1980, and used in 1981, was the Showa Company's new redesigned front fork. The new fork was used on all 1980-1982 models as well as all 1991-1994 models. The fork tubes went from a large tube style to skinny metal tubes with black fork reflector brackets and black metal headlight ears with holes for mounting the headlight and turn signal arms. Because of the new smaller fork tubes, a new fork bridge/triple clamp was used, just like the 1980 model. The rear shocks had chrome lowers with black coil springs and aluminum uppers. The complete exhaust system was black with a black upper shield and this time Honda went with two lower black heat shields. The rear fender, like the previous year came in metal and was painted to match the frame. The wheels and hubs were cloud silver metallic like the previous model year. Just like 1980, the 1981 used a center dash assembly. The dash assembly housed the ignition switch in the bottom right side corner. Above the ignition switch

1981 Tahitian Red CT-70 with all new black mirrors owned by Bill Johnson.

Plastic chrome frame strip, one year only light blue and dark blue main body stickers.

Solid black muffler and heat shield. This design style was used from 1979-1994.

in aluminum without a black rubber tip. The front brake cable as well as the throttle cable came in black like the previous model year. Just like 1980, a black rubber lever cover was used to cover the lever in the control switch. The lever cover was used right up until the end of CT-70 production. The carburetor introduced for 1980 was used again for 1981.

The tail light bracket was black and was used from 1976-1982. It used the same tail light lens as all 1972-1982 model CT-70s. The air cleaner assembly was a carryover design from 1979 with the rubber air breather tube that ran out the top side of the air cleaner canister and through a hole in the frame on the kicker side of the Mini Trail. Just like the previous year, a silver caution label was applied to the top of the air cleaner with black text. The black foot brake pedal was used on all 1980-1982 CT-70s. The turn signals were a two year set up and used from 1981-1982.

Black coil spring rear shocks. Black plastic taillight base with black taillight bracket.

was an amber turn signal indicator light and to the right of it was a green neutral light. Like the previous year, the indicator lights moved to the top right side of the dash assembly from the speedometer. The speedometer made up the entire left side of the dash assembly. The speedometer remained the same as the previous model year. Honda plugged the hole in the frame with a black rubber plug where the ignition mounted on the previous models. A redesigned headlight bucket was used on the 1980 model and it continued onto the next model year. The high beam indicator came in blue and mounted on the top center of the black metal headlight bucket.

As with the 1980 model, the handlebar assembly retained the same BMX-styling with two-piece aluminum risers. The handlebar was new for 1980 and was used again in 1981 and 1982 CT-70. The handlebar controls switched from black to aluminum for 1980-1982, the switches and detail were carried over from the 1980 model. The hand brake lever mounted on the right side of the bike came

The black mirrors were new for 1981 and were used on the 1982 model as well. The box and grid pattern grips that were introduced in 1979 were also used on the 1981. The grips were used on all 1979 to 1982 CT-70s as well as all 1991-1994 CT-70s. New for 1980 was a black metal lower chain guide that mounts to the rear swing arm. It was used from 1980-1982. An all-new seat was issued in 1980 and it would be used on the 1981 and 1982 models as well. The new seat was black vinyl with a slight grain to it with angled piping on each side and a large bright white Honda logo stenciled on the rear of the seat. The bottom of the seat was black painted metal with a storage compartment and a tool-kit holder. Under the seat in the frame was the gas tank, battery, turn signal flasher, wire harness, and rectifier. The battery used was a 6N4-2A-6 Yuasa battery. The horn used on this model was made of metal with eight holes around the outside edges and one in the center. This style horn was used on all 1977-1982 CT-70s. The kicker and shifter came in black. Nineteen-eighty one was the first CT-70 to use hex bolts instead of screws on the engine. The hex bolts were used on all 1981-1994 CT-70s. By years end, a total of 6,089 CT-70s were produced. Two-thousand five hundred and ten less than the previous year.

Tahitian Red plastic front fender and Showa front fork.

BMX style black handlebars. Dash assembly to house speedometer and ignition switch.

Aluminum on/off kill switch assembly, aluminum hand brake lever, and box & grid pattern grips

Rough grain black vinyl seat used on all 1980-1982 U.S.A. models.

Tahitian Red plastic front fender, metal rear fender, and plastic chain guard. Rubber plug to cover ignition switch hole.

Chapter 18

CT-70 1982 Honda

Beginning serial number for all USA models-JH2DD0101BS200002

The 1982 CT-70 was more or less a continuation of the previous model year with a few subtle changes. The new design was part of a three year run for the USA model. Just like the previous year, the 1981 model came in Tahitian Red. The main body decal said "Honda" in black outlined in white and it had a stripe that was white, blue, and black. The stripes were outlined in black with a white outer border. On the shifter side of the frame, just below the seat was a black with white text emissions control warning label. On each side of the frame, on the outside of the fuel tank there were two additional stickers. The shifter side sticker said "Mini Trail 70" and the

The final year of the U.S.A. version of the CT-70 until the re-release in 1991.

Black air cleaner with black round side covers. Black plastic choke lever on carburetor.

Mini Trail 70 badges are stickers rather than stick on aluminum plates. Tahitian Red plastic chain guard.

kicker side sticker had an exhaust warning with tire pressure and vehicle capacity information. The right side sticker was clear with black text. The left side sticker colors matched the main body decal. The front fender came in Tahitian Red and it was made of plastic. This fender was a longer dirt bike style fender compared to the painted original style fender.

New for 1980, and used in 1981, was the Showa Company's new redesigned front fork. The new fork was used on all 1980-1982 models as well as all 1991-1994 models. The fork tubes went from a large tube style to skinny metal tubes with black fork reflector brackets and black metal headlight ears with holes for mounting the headlight and turn signal arms. Because of the new smaller fork tubes, a new fork bridge/triple clamp was used, just like the 1980 model. The rear shocks had chrome lowers with black coil springs and aluminum uppers. The complete exhaust system was black with a black upper shield and this time Honda went with two lower black heat shields. The rear fender, like the previous year came in metal and was painted to match the frame. The wheels and hubs were cloud silver metallic like the previous model year. Just like 1980, the 1981 used a center dash assembly. The dash assembly housed the ignition switch in the bottom right side corner. Above the ignition switch was an amber turn signal indicator light and to the right of it was a green neutral light. Like the previous year, the indicator lights moved to the top right side of the dash assembly from the speedometer. The speedometer made up the entire left side of the dash assembly. The speedometer remained the same as the previous model year. Honda plugged the hole in the frame with a black rubber plug where the ignition mounted on the previous models. A redesigned headlight bucket was used on the 1980 model and it continued onto the next model year. The high beam indicator came in blue and mounted on the top center of the black metal headlight bucket.

As with the 1980 model, the handlebar assembly retained the same BMX-styling with two-piece aluminum risers. The handlebar was new for 1980 and was used again in 1981 and 1982 CT-70. The handlebar controls switched from black to aluminum for 1980-1982, the switches and detail were carried over from the 1980 model. The hand brake lever mounted on the right side of the bike came in aluminum without a black rubber tip. The front brake cable as well as the throttle cable came in black like the previous model year. Just like 1980, a black rubber lever cover was used to cover the lever in the control switch. The lever cover was used right up until the end of CT-70 production. The carburetor introduced for 1980 was used again for 1981.

The tail light bracket was black and was used from 1976-1982. It used the same tail light lens as all 1972-1982 model CT-70s. The air cleaner assembly was a carryover design from 1979 with the rubber air breather tube that ran out the top side of the air cleaner canister and through a hole in the frame on the kicker side of the Mini Trail. Just like the previous year, a silver caution label was applied to the top of the air cleaner with black text. The black foot brake pedal was used on all 1980-1982 CT-70s. The turn signals were a two year set up and used from 1981-1982.

The black mirrors were new for 1981 and were used on the 1982 model as well. The box and grid pattern grips that were introduced in 1979 were also used on the 1981. The

High beam indicator located in the top of the headlight and not the speedometer.

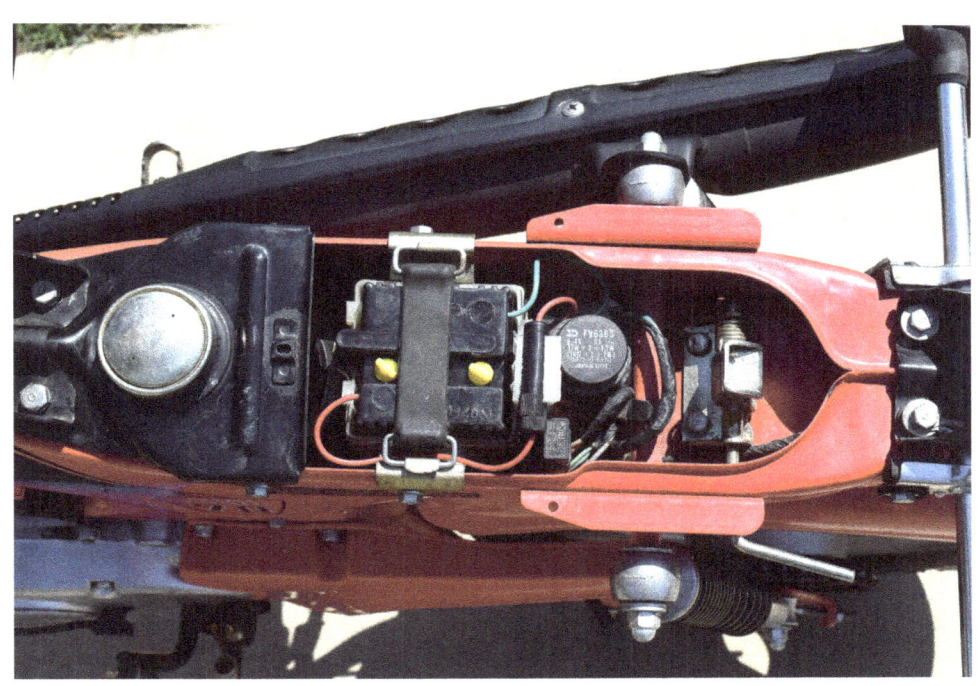

Yuasa battery, product code 6N4-2A-6.

Aluminum on/off kill switch with mirror mount and brake lever mount.

Aluminum switch with horn, hi/low, and turn signal controls.

grips were used on all 1979 to 1982 CT-70s as well as all 1991-1994 CT-70s. New for 1980 was a black metal lower chain guide that mounts to the rear swing arm. It was used from 1980-1982. An all-new seat was issued in 1980 and it would be used on the 1981 and 1982 models as well. The new seat was black vinyl with a slight grain to it with angled piping on each side and a large bright white Honda logo stenciled on the rear of the seat. The bottom of the seat was black painted metal with a storage compartment and a tool-kit holder. Under the seat in the frame was the gas tank, battery, turn signal flasher, wire harness, and rectifier. The battery used was a 6N4-2A-6 Yuasa battery. The horn used on this model was made of metal with eight holes around the outside edges and one in the center. This style horn was used on all 1977-1982 CT-70s. The kicker and shifter came in black. Nineteen-eighty one was the first CT-70 to use hex bolts instead of screws on the engine. The hex bolts were used on all 1981-1994 CT-70s. By years end, a total of 6,089 CT-70s were produced. Two-thousand five hundred and ten less than the previous year.

72cc engine with three-speed up shift transmission.

Chapter 19

CT-70 1983 - 1986 Honda Canada Only

For whatever reason, Honda decided to drop the CT-70 line for U.S.A. production at the end of the 1982 model year. Sales declined and the three-wheeler craze was sweeping the nation and that may have contributed to the decline.

Between 1983 and 1986, Honda built CT-70s for Canada only. They closely resembled the 1980-1982 U.S.A version and remained a six-volt system. The main body decals changed from year to year but other styling features and components remained the same including the color. All 1983-1985 Canadian CT-70s came with silver wheels. The speedometers were significant to the Canadian models, being that they read in Kilometers per hour instead

1985 Canadian CT-70 owned by Jesse Kimball of Grand Marais Minnesota.

Original turn signals removed for trail riding, a common occurrence with Trail 70s. Most features remained the same as the 1980-1982 U.S.A versions.

of miles per hour. The 1980-1982 U.S.A. models topped out at 50 mph on the speedometers and the Canadian versions topped out at 80 Km/h.

Nineteen eighty-six was the last year of the CT-70 built for the Canadian market. Later it was brought back in 1991 with a Canadian and U.S.A version. The Canadian and U.S.A. versions of the CT-70 ended production in 1994. Very few people have ever seen a 1986 CT-70 or know they exist. Ryan Hoffman of Canada has come across a few, but never any quality ones. Ryan owns an original sales brochure and one glimpse at it and you will want to own one! The red, white, and blue main body decal stands out and the most eye catching part of the motorcycle is the gold wheels, hubs, and brake plates. The three wheelers of the 1980s as well as the 1986 Z50R have gold wheels and today collectors go crazy over finding a Honda with gold wheels.

Original 1986 dealer sales brochure owned by Ryan Hoffman of Alberta Canada.

102

Chapter 20

CT-70 1991 Honda

Serial number range for California models- JH2DB011MS000007-JH2DB011MS000645
Serial number for all other USA models-JH2DB010MS000005-JH2DB010MS002310
Engine serial number range for both California and other USA States- DB01E-2000001-
Three Speed Auto Clutch, 72cc Overhead Cam Engine
Carburetor Serial number California models-PB12E A and non-California models are PB12D A

The rebirth of an American Legend

After an eight-year hiatus, Honda brought back the bike that so many of us grew up loving. I can remember waiting for the release of this bike like it was yesterday. I remember reading about the re-release in Dirt Bike Magazine, and I could not wait to get a brochure, and most importantly, sit on one at my local dealership.

With eight years past and even more years since the first model was released, many people waited in anticipation and wondered what a modern version of a classic Mini Trail would look like. Keeping with the 1980s models, the new version came in Italian Red paint. For the first

The re-released 1991 Honda CT-70.

Emissions canister used in conjunction with the specially designed carburetor installed on all California models.

time ever in CT-70 history, the new release came with Ross White painted rims, and keeping with tradition the rims and hubs had the same design style as the first model CT-70. The hubs, and brake plates also came in Ross White. The mounting hardware on the wheels were finished with grade-eight bolts and front and rear brake arms came with zinc coating. The rims carried Bridgestone Trail Wing 3 on/off road tires. The bolts that mount the hubs in the rim halves are 12mm and the bolts that hold the rim halves together are 10mm. The rim halves have different size holes to accept the bolts. These rims were only used on the 1991 CT-70.

A BMX-style handle bar was used; a trend that started with the 1979 model and it too came in black to match the triple clamp, black rubber grips, and bar risers. Just like the previous models, each side of the bar featured control switches. The right bar featured the on/off kill switch in black with a red twist knob. The left bar featured a control switch that was comprised of the hi-low beam switch, horn button, and turn signal controls and like the right side switch it too came in black.

The front fork came with chrome upper tubes with aluminum lower shock tubes. Large round amber reflectors were mounted on each fork leg for road safety regulations and the lower shifter side fork leg featured a black mounting bracket to hold the black wire cable bracket. Black headlight mounting ears were mounted on the upper fork legs to house the large Italian Red headlight bucket. Turn signal arm brackets sat below the headlight bracket ears and just like those brackets, they came in black. The turn signals were black plastic with square amber lenses.

The rear shocks came with black coil springs without shock covers and aluminum tops and bottoms. Black throttle and front brake cables were used on the all-new model, a feature that dates back to the 1976 model year. Keeping up with the times, the 1991 CT-70 lacked the chrome that the early bikes were known for - the black exhaust system with a three-piece black heat shield is a good examples of the new look. A black kicker and shifter were used to go along with the black European style center stand assembly and foot brake pedal. Large black rubber padded foot pegs were mounted on a sturdy black step bar assembly. The large fold-up rubber foot pegs were a new feature in the world of CT-70's, a design that made its debut in 1972 on the Z50A. Honda did away with the engine crash guard in 1979 and they did not bring it back for the next generation either. The frame holes for the upper engine crash guard were used for the wire harness wire bracket on the kicker side.

A new feature for 1991 was a steering fork stop that was outfitted with a fork lock as an anti-theft deterrent. The main body decals were slanted stripes in Yellow with the word "Honda" cut out of it in silver, and "CT-70" in White. According to the parts books a "Pure" Red front and an "Italian" rear fender were used. The front fender was plastic and the rear was painted metal. Nineteen-ninety one was the first model to lack the frame badges that mounted just below the center of the seat. The stamped indentations in the frame were left blank. A large Cloud Silver flywheel cover that served as a partial chain guard was used on the newly released model. A continuation of the 1980 model was a black rubber hand brake lever cover. This was used on all 1980-1994 CT-70s. All 1991-1994 CT-70s came with black aluminum brake levers without a rubber tip on the end. For the first time ever Honda went with an upper chain guard in black and a lower chain guard in white plastic.

The 1991 model brought back two, first-generation features. The first was the main body-mounted ignition switch and the second was a speedometer integrated into the headlight bucket. Just like the fenders, rear swing arm, and frame, the headlight bucket also came in Italian Red. A large black plastic taillight assembly with turn signals mounted to it graced the back end of the trail 70 with a bold new style. Dating back to the 1979 model, the seat on the 1991 stuck with the same design with a rough grain seat cover with no ribs or pleats on the top of the cover. Piping ran at an angle at the back of the seat and at the front.

1991 was the only 1990s CT-70 to have yellow and silver stripe stickers on the main body. Center stand and long black plastic upper chain guard and a small white plastic chain guard.

A bold Honda logo finished off the back of the seat in white. Just like all of the previous models, the seat flipped forward. The unique thing about the 1990 seats is that you needed a key to unlock the seat and it had spring-loaded pegs in the rear. Under the seat, you could find the YT4L-BS code Yuasa battery, gas tank/cap, and a toolbox compartment. The toolbox compartment secured the tools inside a plastic compartment unlike the original version, which was in a metal sleeve secured with a metal clip. On the shifter side of the Mini Trail a helmet lock was present, a feature that was last used on the 1978 model.

An interesting feature on the 1991 CT70 is the evaporative emission canister assembly; this was the first time this was used on a trail 70. The tube for this unit exited out the bottom of the frame and was mounted to the right side of the rear swing arm. It was used on all 1991-1994 models that were sold in California. The carburetor for the California models was also different because of this emission canister set up. The ignition and wiring system on this model consisted of a C.D.I module. As mentioned earlier, the ignition switch and battery, ignition coil, and a regulator/rectifier by the Shindengen Company of Japan were also used. A new carburetor was introduced for 1991 and it would be used on all 1991-1994 models. It resembled the carburetor of the late 1970s and early 80s with the round bottom bowl and the plastic choke lever.

For safety as well as informative purposes, the all-new generation of the CT-70 was outfitted with many decals. The Honda parts books gives part numbers for several decals, however not all of them have been present on all motorcycles from the factory or even when pictured in dealer brochures. I will explain the Honda recommendations for decals per the parts books. The upper chain guard came with a tire pressure as well as a drive chain instructional decal. Under the seat by the gas cap, there was an "unleaded fuel recommended" decal. A yellow with black text "helmet holder" decal was placed next to the helmet holder under the seat. A white with black text color code label was placed under the seat on the frame on the kicker side of the motorcycle. A transparent decal with Championship White text was placed on top of the headlight bucket that stated: "Operator only-No passengers." A top of frame decal with the "Honda Wing" was placed in front of the seat on the kicker side. A warning label was placed just above the back of the flywheel cover on the frame. These decals are recommended for use on all 1991-1994 models.

After one year of production, sales were low. Six-hundred and thirty-eight California serial number models were produced and two-thousand three hundred and five were produced for the other forty-nine states, bringing total production to a dismal two-thousand nine hundred and forty three.

Full black exhaust system. Large "Pure Red" plastic front fender. Ross white wheels and hubs

Chapter 21
CT-70 1992 Honda

Beginning serial number for California models-JH2DB011NK100001
Beginning serial number for all other USA models-JH2DB010NK100001

Just like the previous year, the 1992 model came with Ross White painted rims, hubs, and brake plates. The mounting hardware on the wheels were finished with grade eight bolts and front and rear brake arms were coated in zinc plating. Bridgestone supplied the rubber, Trail Wing 3 on/off road tires.

A BMX-style handle bar was used, a trend that started with the 1979 model, and it too came in black to match the triple clamp, black rubber grips, and bar risers. Just like the previous models, each side of the bar featured control switches. The right bar featured the on/off kill switch in black with a red twist knob. The left bar featured

Large speedometer with the neutral, high beam, and turn signal lights integrated in the face.

a control switch that was comprised of the hi-low beam switch, horn button, and turn signal controls, and like the right side switch it too came in black. The front fork came with chrome upper tubes with aluminum lower shock tubes. Large round amber reflectors were mounted on each fork leg to meet road safety regulations, and the lower shifter side fork leg featured a black mounting bracket to hold the black wire cable bracket.

The large Italian Red headlight bucket headlight housing came with black ears that mounted to the upper fork legs. Turn signal arm brackets sat below the headlight bracket ears, and just like those brackets, they came in black. The turn signals were black plastic with square amber lenses. The rear shocks came with black coil springs without shock covers and aluminum tops and bottoms. Black throttle and front brake cables were used on the all-new model; a feature that dates back to the 1976 model year. Keeping with the times, the 1992 CT-70 lacked the chrome seen on the early bikes. The black exhaust system used a three-piece black heat shield. A black kicker and shifter were used to go along with the black European style center stand assembly and foot brake pedal. Large black rubber padded foot pegs were mounted on a sturdy black step bar assembly. The large fold-up rubber foot pegs were a new

12 volt C.D.I. 72cc engine with a three speed up shift pattern transmission.

feature in the world of CT-70s, a design that made its debut in 1972 on the Z50A.

Honda did away with the engine crash guard in 1979 and they did not bring it back for the next generation either. The frame holes for the upper engine crash guard were used for the wire harness wire bracket. A new feature for 1991 was a steering fork stop that was outfitted with a fork lock as an anti-theft deterrent. The main body decals were slanted stripes in Purple with the word "Honda" cut out of it and the lower stripe was blue-green. A separate decal below the bottom stripe said "CT-70" in White. A Pure Red front and an Italian rear fender were used, just like the previous model. The front fender was plastic and the rear was painted metal. 1991 was the first model to lack the frame badges that were mounted just below the center of the seat. Instead the stamped indentations in the frame were left blank - and the 1992 model continued on with this tradition. Honda did away with the plastic top-of-the-frame molding and brought back the chrome molding for 1991. This molding was used on all 1991-1994 CT70s.

A large Cloud Silver flywheel cover that served as a partial chain guard was used on the newly released model. For the first time

Large black plastic upper chain guard, and a small white plastic lower chain guard.

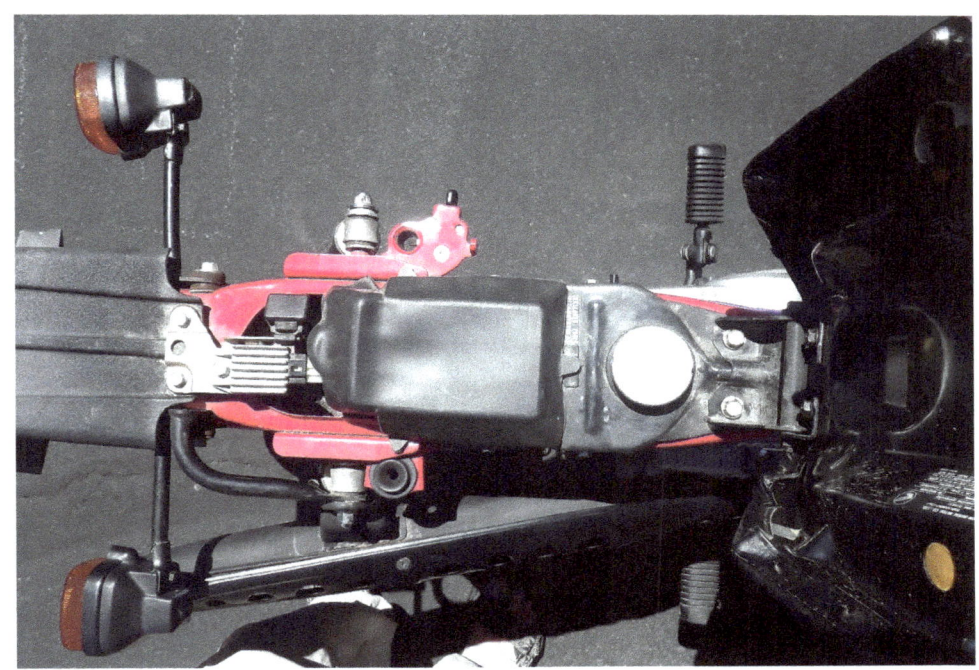

Black plastic turn signals with black metal mounting arms. Large rubber fold up foot pegs.

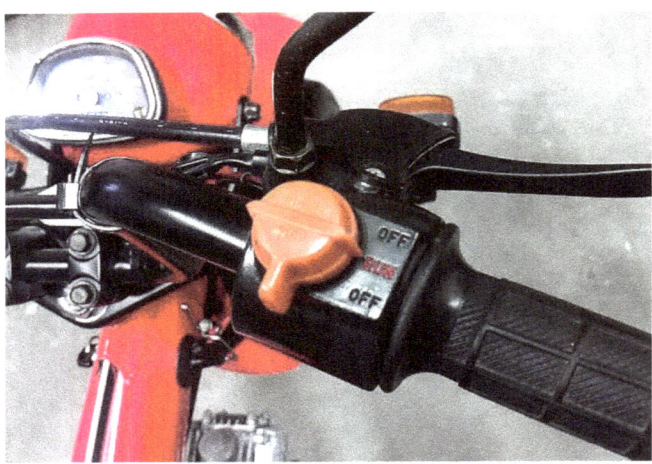

Black on/off kill switch with orange twist knob. Box and grid pattern grips and black metal brake lever with black rubber lever cover.

Black hi/low switch with horn and turn signal indicator switch.

Ross white wheels and hub.

ever Honda went with an upper chain guard in black metal and a lower chain guard in white plastic. The 1991 model brought back two, first generation features and they carried over to the 1992 model year. The first was the main body mounted ignition switch and the second was a speedometer integrated into the headlight bucket. A large black plastic taillight assembly, with turn signals mounted to it, graced the back end of the Trail 70 with a bold new style. Dating back to the 1979 model, the seat on the 1992 stuck with the same design, which featured a rough grain seat cover without ribs or pleats on the top of the cover. Piping ran at an angle at the back of the seat and at the front. A bold Honda logo finished off the back of the seat in white. Just like all of the previous models, the seat flipped forward. Under the seat, you could find the YT4L-BS code Yuasa battery, gas tank/cap, and a toolbox compartment. The seat came with a locking system, a feature that was all-new for the 1991 model and carried over to the 1992 model. On the shifter side of the Mini Trail, a helmet lock was present, a feature that had not been used since the 1978 model. An interesting feature on the 1992 CT70 is the evaporative emission canister assembly. It was a carryover item from the previous year. The tube for this unit exited out the bottom of the frame and was mounted to the right side of the rear swing arm. It was used on all 1991-1994 California models and a different carburetor was used with it.

The ignition and wiring system on this model consisted of a C.D.I module. As mentioned earlier, the ignition switch and battery, ignition coil, and a regulator/rectifier from the Shindengen Company of Japan were used. For safety as well informative purposes the all-new generation of the CT70 was outfitted with many decals. The Honda parts books give part numbers for the following decals, however not all of them have been present on all motorcycles from the factory or even when pictured in dealer brochures. The upper chain guard came with a tire pressure as well as a drive chain instructional decal. Under the seat by the gas cap, there was an "unleaded fuel recommended" decal. A yellow with black text "helmet holder decal was place next to the helmet holder under the seat. A white with black text color code label was placed under the seat on the frame on the kicker side of the motorcycle. A transparent decal with Championship white text was placed on top of the headlight bucket that stated, "Operator only-No passengers." A top-of-frame decal with the "Honda Wing" was placed in front of the seat on the kicker side. A warning label was placed just above the back of the flywheel cover on the frame. These decals are recommended for use on all 1991-1994 models.

One might think that after the re-release of the CT70 in 1991 that sales would climb for the next year, but that was hardly the case. Sales dropped by 799 overall bikes. Three-hundred and eighty-three California models were produced and only 1,761 for the remaining 49 states. With sales decreasing, one could probably predict what was going to happen to the model that sold like crazy in the early 1970's. However, this would not be the last model produced. Plans were in the works for another run and the consumer could go out and purchase a 1993 CT-70.

Carburetor used on all 1992 models except the California models.

Chapter 22

CT-70 1993 Honda

Beginning serial number for California models-JH2DB011PK200001
Beginning serial number for all other USA models-JH2DB010PK200001

The 1993 bikes, just like the two previous years, came with Ross White painted rims, hubs, and brake plates. The mounting hardware on the wheels was finished with grade eight bolts and front and rear brake arms with zinc coating. The rims carried Bridgestone Trail Wing 3 on/off road tires. A BMX-style handle bar was used; a trend that started with the 1979 model and it too came in black to match the triple clamp, black rubber grips, and bar risers. Just like the previous models, each side of the bar featured control switches. The right bar featured the on/off kill switch in black with a red twist knob. The left bar featured a control switch that was comprised of the hi-low beam switch, horn button,

and turn signal controls and like the right side switch it too came in black.

The front fork came with chrome upper tubes with aluminum lower shock tubes. Large round amber reflectors were mounted on each fork leg for road safety regulations and the lower shifter side fork leg featured a black mounting bracket to hold the black wire cable bracket. An Italian Red headlight bucket with black ears, bolted to the upper fork legs. Turn signal arm brackets were located below the headlight bracket ears and, just like those brackets, they came in black. The turn signals used black plastic housings with square amber lenses. The rear shocks came with black coil springs without shock covers and aluminum tops and bottoms. Black throttle and front brake cables were used on the all-new model; a feature that dates back to the 1976 model year. Keeping up with the times, the 1993 CT lacked the chrome that the early bikes were so well known for. The entire exhaust system came in black, including the three-piece heat shield. A kicker and shifter were both black to match the black European style center stand assembly and foot brake pedal. Large black rubber padded foot pegs were mounted on a sturdy black step bar assembly. The large fold-up rubber foot pegs were a new feature in the world of CT-70s, a design that made its debut in 1972 on the Z50A.

As mentioned earlier, Honda did away with the

1993 CT-70 owned by Bill Johnson. Purple and teal main body decals were used 1992-1994.

Black headlight mounting brackets and a fork lock.

Seat bottom with tool compartment mounted up top in a plastic container.

engine crash guard in 1979 and they did not bring it back for the next generation. The frame holes for the upper engine crash guard were used for the wire harness wire bracket. A steering fork stop with a fork lock as an anti-theft deterrent was used on all 1991-1994 models. Just like the previous year, the main body decals consisted of slanted stripes. The top stripe was Purple with the word "Honda" cut out of it and the lower stripe was blue-green. A separate decal below the bottom stripe said "CT-70" in White. A "Cherry" Red front and an "Italian" rear fender were used. The front fender was plastic and the rear was painted metal. Just like the previous two models, the 1993 lacked the frame badges that were mounted just below the center of the seat and the frame indentations were left blank. A large Cloud Silver flywheel cover that served as a partial chain guard was used on the newly released model.

For the first time ever, Honda went with an upper chain guard in black and a lower chain guard in white plastic. The 1993 model continued with two first generation features. The first was the main-body mounted ignition switch and the second was a speedometer integrated into the headlight bucket. Just like the fenders, rear swing arm, and frame the headlight bucket also came in Italian Red. A large black plastic taillight assembly with turn signals mounted to it graced the back end of the trail 70 with a bold new style. Dating back to the 1979 model, the seat on the 1993 stuck with the same

Black plastic taillight bracket, full black exhaust system, and black turn signal arms and signals.

Black bars, triple clamp, bar risers, cables, headlight mounts, and turn signals.

Black hi/low and turn signal control switch.

Black on/off switch with mirror and brake lever mounts. Box and grid pattern grip.

Ross White wheels, Bridgestone Trail Wing 3 tires, and "Cherry Red" front fender.

design with a rough grain seat cover with no ribs or pleats on the top of the cover. Piping ran at an angle at the back of the seat and at the front. A bold Honda logo finished off the back of the seat in white. Just like all of the previous models, the seat flipped forward. Under the seat, you could find the YT4L-BS code Yuasa battery, gas tank/cap, and a toolbox compartment.

The 1993 seat came with a locking system, a feature that was used on all 1991-1994 models. On the shifter side of the Mini Trail, a helmet lock was present, a feature that was last was used on the 1978 model. Just like the previous 2 years, the 1993 CT-70 came with an Evaporative Emission Canister Assembly. The tube for this unit exited out the bottom of the frame and was mounted to the right side of the rear swing arm. It was used on 1991-1994 California models. A special carburetor was used to go with the canister emission system. The ignition and wiring system on this model consisted of a C.D.I module, the ignition switch and battery, an ignition coil, and a regulator/rectifier by the Shindengen Company of Japan.

For safety as well as informative purposes the all-new generation of the CT-70 was outfitted with many decals. The Honda parts books gives part numbers for the following decals, however not all of them have been present on all motorcycles from the facztory or even when pictured in dealer brochures. I will explain the Honda recommendations for decals per the parts books. The upper chain guard came with a tire pressure as well as a drive chain instructional decal. Under the seat by the gas cap, there was an "unleaded fuel recommended" decal. A yellow with black text "helmet holder decal was place next to the helmet holder under the seat. A white with black text color code label was placed under the seat on the frame on the kicker side of the motorcycle. A transparent decal with Championship white text was placed on top of the headlight bucket that stated, "Operator only-No passengers." A top of frame decal with the "Honda Wing" was placed in front of the seat on the kicker side. A warning label was placed just above the back of the flywheel cover on the frame. These decals are recommended for use on all 1991-1994 models.

No productions numbers have been reported, however I have photographed serial number 3,443.

Black coil spring rear shocks without shock top covers, black plastic taillight bracket with lens and reflector.

Chapter 23
CT-70 1994 Honda

Beginning serial number for California models-JH2DB011RK300001
Beginning serial number for all other USA models- JH2DB010RK300001

The 1994 CT-70 would be the final CT-70 for the U.S.A market. Ross White painted rims, hubs, and brake plates were used one final time. The mounting hardware on the wheels were finished with grade eight bolts and front and rear brake arms in zinc coating. The rims came with Bridgestone Trail Wing 3 on/off road tires. The same BMX-style handlebar was used from the previous 3 years.

The right bar featured the on/off kill switch in black with a red twist knob. The left bar featured a control switch that was comprised of the hi-low beam switch, horn button, and turn signal controls and like the right side switch it too came in black. The front fork came with chrome upper tubes with aluminum lower shock tubes. Large round amber reflectors were mounted on each fork leg for road

1994, the final year CT-70 produced.

Helmet lock and seat latch-locking assembly.

safety regulations and the lower shifter side fork leg featured a black mounting bracket to hold the black wire cable bracket. Black headlight mounting ears were mounted on the upper fork legs to house the large Italian Red headlight bucket. Turn signal arm brackets sat below the headlight bracket ears and just like those brackets; they came in black as well. The turn signals were black plastic with square amber lenses. The rear shocks came with black coil springs without shock covers and aluminum tops and bottoms. The cables were black like the previous year.

The main body decals were the same as the 1993 model. A "Cherry" Red front and an "Italian" red rear fender was used. The front fender was plastic and the rear was painted metal. 1991-1994 models lacked the frame badges that were mounted just below the center of the seat and the stamped indentations in the frame were left blank. A large Cloud Silver flywheel cover that served as a partial chain guard was used on the newly released model. For the first time ever Honda went with an upper chain guard in metal painted black and a lower chain guard in white plastic. The 1994 model, just like the previous three years, brought back two first-generation features. The first was the main-body mounted ignition switch, and the second was a speedometer integrated into the headlight bucket. Just like the fenders, rear swing arm, and frame, the headlight bucket also came in Italian Red. A large black plastic taillight assembly with turn signals mounted to it graced the back end of the Trail 70 with a bold new style.

The seat was identical to the previous model. Piping ran at an angle at the back of the seat and at the front. A bold Honda logo finished off the back of the seat in white. Just like all of the previous models, the seat flipped forward. Under the seat, you could find the YT4L-BS code Yuasa battery, gas tank/cap, and toolbox compartment. The seat came with a locking system, a feature that was used on the '91-'94 models. On the shifter side of the Mini Trail a helmet lock was present; a feature that was last used on the 1978 model. Just like the previous model, the 1994 has the Evaporative Emission Canister Assembly. The tube for this unit exited out the bottom of the frame and was mounted to the right side of the rear swing arm. It was used on all California models along with a special carburetor. The ignition and wiring system on this model consisted of a C.D.I module. As mentioned earlier, the ignition switch and battery, ignition coil, and a regulator/rectifier by the Shindengen Company of Japan were also used on this model.

A complete black exhaust system with a three-piece black heat shield set kept the exhaust system covered. A black kicker and shifter were used to go along with the black European style center stand assembly and foot brake pedal. Large black rubber padded foot pegs were mounted on a sturdy black step bar assembly. The large fold up rubber foot pegs were a new feature in the world of CT70s, a design that made its debut in 1972 on the Z50A K3. Honda did away with the engine crash guard in 1979 and they did not bring it back for the next generation model either. The frame holes for the upper engine crash guard were used for the wire harness wire bracket. A new feature for 1991-1994 models was a steering fork stop that was outfitted with a fork lock as an anti-theft feature.

For safety as well informative purposes, the all-new generation of the CT-70 was outfitted with many decals. The Honda parts books gives part numbers for several decals, however not all of them have been present on all motorcycles from the factory or even when pictured in dealer brochures. I will explain the Honda recommendations for

Large speedometer integrated into the headlight bucket like the first model CT-70s. High beam, neutral, and turn signal indicators are present in the faceplate.

decals per the parts books. The upper chain guard came with a tire pressure as well as a drive chain instructional decal. Under the seat by the gas cap, there was an "unleaded fuel recommended" decal. A yellow with black text "helmet holder" decal was placed next to the helmet holder under the seat. A white with black text color code label was placed under the seat on the frame on the kicker side of the motorcycle. A transparent decal with Championship white text was placed on top of the headlight bucket that stated, "Operator only-No passengers." A top of frame decal with the "Honda Wing" was placed in front of the seat on the kicker side. A warning label was placed just above the back of the flywheel cover on the frame. These decals are recommended for use on all 1991-1994 models.

After four short years of production, sales were not what Honda had hoped for, though Honda did not provide actual production numbers. Production for the USA version of one of America's greatest motorcycles ended. Just about the time the CT-70 production ended is about the time that vintage CT-70s started showing up on eBay for sale. The collector hobby started to boom in the mid-1990s and specialty parts distributors started selling replacement parts. Over the last ten years or so, more and more aftermarket parts have become available, as O.E.M. replacement parts have been discontinued and N.O.S. parts are rare and difficult to find.

Even though CT-70 production ceased in 1994, the popularity of this particular model exploded and continues to be one of the most popular restored Mini Trails, if not the most popular! Engine builder Tim Lavoi is amazed by the amount of interest in the CT-70. "Eighty to ninety percent of the engines I rebuild are from CT-70s," explains Tim. "I continue to build on a daily basis for individual clients as well as many specialty parts websites and restoration shops like Mike's Mini Trails and Stewart's Cycles and ATV's. TB Parts and Northeast Vintage Cycle keep me stocked up on engine parts. There never seems to be a shortage of work!"

Black air cleaner with chrome end covers. Used 1991-1994.

Chapter 24
SL-70 1971-1972 Honda

Beginning Serial number 1000001

By 1971, Honda had the CL-70, the CT-70, and along came the SL-70 Motorsport. The all-new SL-70 was a street and trail mini motorcycle. It came with a four-stroke engine, a four- speed manual hand clutch transmission, and a full-cradle frame. Production ran from 1971 to 1973.

The first model SL-70 production ran from 1971 to 1972 and it came in three superb color options. You had a choice of Summer Yellow, Aquarius Blue, and Light Ruby Red. The headlight bucket, front fender bracket, front fender, rear fender, fuel tank, and both side covers came in the main body color. The fenders and the headlight bucket were metal and the side covers were molded

An Aquarius Blue 1st model SL-70 Motorsport owned by Greg Griffin of Minnesota.

A double cradle pipe frame in cloud silver. 72cc engine with a four-speed manual transmission

plastic. The side covers had SL 70 stickers. "SL" was blue with a white outline, "70" was red with a white outline, and the entire sticker had a black background with a white star between "SL & 70". The fuel tank had a large white teardrop on each side with a white pin stripe above it on the Light Ruby Red and Aquarius Blue motorcycles. The same paint design was black if the motorcycle was Summer Yellow. All three colors had a Blue "Honda" stick-on emblem that had chrome boarders and black in the background. The gas cap was flat, with knurled edges, and it came in chrome.

The double cradle pipe frame was painted Cloud Silver and the engine hanger plate set, according to Honda parts books, was painted Dark Silver Metallic. A two and three quarter inch by fourteen-inch knobby rear tire and a two and a half inch by sixteen-inch knobby front tire for better handling came on all SL-70s. Bridgestone and Nitto tires were used on the SL-70. Both front and rear wheels came with spokes and aluminum hubs. Small chrome brackets that mounted to the fork tubes held on the front fork reflectors and they attached to the sides of the headlight bucket. They were the same as the small reflectors used on the first model CT-70. The difference between these reflectors was that they did not require a black rubber-mounting base but rather a headlight case setting stay bolt. The headlight unit was the same as the CL-70 K1, CT-70 K1, and XL and XL K1. The seat used on the SL-70 was also used on the SL-70 K1 and the first model XL-70.

The seat was black vinyl, with a silver Honda logo centered on the back of the seat. Nine heat pressed seams and a full piping band around the top edge of the seat finished it off. Below the seat, the chrome license plate bracket mounted to the rear fender. Of note, it was only used on the first model SL-70. The taillight and lens were also used on the first model CT-70. On the left side of the motorcycle was a flywheel cover in Cloud Silver paint with a polished aluminum points cover that said "Honda Made in Japan". Adjoining the flywheel cover was a chain guard and together they took care of the shifter side of the motorcycle. The chain guard came in semi glazed black paint. The clutch cover on the kicker side of the motorcycle was also cloud silver and it had oil instructions in raised letters on the top left cover of the cover. There was also a polished removable clutch cover held on by two Phillips head screws. Unlike the other 72cc motorcycles in the Honda line up, the SL-70 had the foot pegs mounted directly to the frame without a separate foot peg assembly. The pegs had springs for easy fold up capabilities and they

2.5 x 16 inch knobby front tire in either Bridgestone or Nitto.

2.75 x 14 knobby rear tire in either Bridgestone or Nitto.

Chrome license plate frame and taillight bracket mounted on a metal painted rear fender in Aquarius Blue.

Large chrome motocross style handlebars and an Aquarius Blue headlight shell with a chrome trim ring.

A low up swept muffler in high heat black with a small chrome heat shield.

had large rubbers to keep the riders feet in place. The kickstand was mounted directly to the bottom side of the frame on the shifter side.

The exhaust system is unique on the SL-70. It sweeps low below the engine and the foot peg on the kicker side before turning up in the back. The complete exhaust system came in flat black high-temperature paint. A small chrome heat shield was fastened to the muffler with two Philips head screws. The muffler guard was simple; it came in chrome and had just two, long horizontal cutouts for cooling. Besides the front hand brake, a rear foot brake pedal was mounted to the frame for rear stopping power. The rear brake rod was mounted behind the frame and attached to the rear brake arm. Besides a headlight and taillight, a frame-mounted on/off ignition switch completed the electrical side of the SL-70. The ignition switch was unique to the first model SL.

The cylinder and cylinder head were both silver, unlike the CT-70, which had a cylinder painted black. An on/off/reserve petcock fuel valve was mounted on the shifter side of the motorcycle to the bottom of the fuel tank and it made transporting the motorcycle a breeze. The Sl-70 came with an "off black" colored air cleaner assembly. The air cleaner had round chrome caps on each side and this particular air cleaner was only used on the first model SL-70. For carburetion, the SL-70 used a carburetor with the same top set as the CL-70. This particular carburetor was used on all SL and XL 70s. The handlebar used on the SL-70 line was a true wide motocross style bar. The bar came in chrome and it had a clutch lever on the left side and a front brake lever on the right side. The bar was mounted to the top of the forks with a dark silver metallic fork-top bridge that held two aluminum handlebar holder risers. The left side of the handlebar had a mount for the clutch lever and a plug in the bar for a horn, which the first model SL-70 did not have. The right side of the bar also had a mount for the lever perch as well as an aluminum on/off kill switch with a low and high beam lever below that. The right side control switch was used on all SL-70s. Both lever mounts had holes to mount chrome mirrors for street legal action.

The first model SL-70 did not have a speedometer; however it was an optional item available from the dealer. The front hub had the mount for the cable, and the bracket in front of the bars that held the high beam indicator could be removed before attaching the optional one-year only speedometer (the speedo came with an integral high beam indicator). The speedometer case was black with a chrome trim ring around the top edge. The face was black with white hash marks and numbers. The top speed was sixty miles per hour. The bottom of the speedometer said "Nippon Seiki Japan". To install the speedo, the owner only had to follow the simple instructions: First, the factory high beam mounting bracket needs to be removed. Be sure to use the factory bracket that came with the speedometer, for proper fitment. The outer corners of the bracket have holes and they attach to the upper fork tube bolts.

A chrome kicker and shifter were used and both had ribbed rubber pieces to limit slipping by the rider's feet. The orange rectifier and battery used in the first model SL-70 was the same as the first model CT70. The battery installed was 6N2A-2C. The Coil used in the SL-70 was unique and only used on the SL-70. The spark plug cap had an "HM" logo signifying Honda made it. It came in black with a black coil wire, and mounted under the fuel tank on the kicker side of the motorcycle. The wire harness was gray and was unique to the first model SL-70. On the kick-starter side of the motorcycle just behind the kick-starter was a black brake light switch. The brake light switch was used on all SL-70s, XL-70s, and the first model CT-90.

The rear of the motorcycle had a tubular swing arm and a rear brake stopper arm that attached to the rear brake plate and the frame. A forty-four-tooth rear sprocket and a ninety-two-link chain powered the rear wheel on the SL-70. The front fork had chrome uppers with aluminum lowers separated by black rubber dust seal caps. The front suspension was made up of coil springs like the rear suspension. All early first-model SL-70s used the rear shocks that had aluminum tops and bottoms with chrome coil springs. According to Honda parts books, later in the production run at serial 1037835 they switched over to a longer shock that had steel on the lower portion instead of aluminum.

You cannot always trust the parts books as I have found during my extensive research with Honda Mini Trail Z50s. The best way to figure out the running changes are to document original bikes. Randy Marble has done just that, and here is the information he has provided. "The one known running change that Honda made during the manufacturing process of the SL-70 K0 was the

9 seam black vinyl seat with 4 chrome buttons.

Both lever mounts have holes to mount chrome mirrors for street legal action. Right side bar mounted kill switch with red twist knob.

Plastic removable battery side cover with Blue and Red SL70 sticker. Fold up foot pegs, and frame bracket to mount the kickstand.

style of the rear shocks. First up was a shock that was very similar to that of the CT70, but without the body-colored top cover. Second generation is a sleeker, longer lower shock body with a retaining ring for the spring. Current research shows that Honda made the shock change somewhere between VIN# 38369 and 43709."

The handle grips were black with a rectangular pattern of raised pieces of rubber across the entire grip for rider ventilation. This style grip was used on the entire SL line of motorcycles from the SL-70 to the SL-350. The clutch, throttle, and front brake cable came in gray. Aluminum hand brake levers with black rubber tips were used on all SL-70s. From the factory, a thin layer of clear protective film was put onto the brake levers. When looking over original brake levers with the clear protective coating you may find that they are yellowed, cracked, torn, or missing completely. The top of the tank had a clear sticker with Championship White writing that said, "Remember-Preserve Nature-Always wear a helmet - think safety." The clear and white sticker came on the Aquarius Blue and the Light Ruby red models. If the motorcycle was Summer Yellow, it came with a clear sticker with black text.

The chain guard had a tire pressure decal in black with silver text. On the down tube on the muffler side of the frame just above the muffler, a silver decal with black text was stuck to the frame to let the rider know about the USDA approved spark arrestor exhaust. The V.I.N tag was mounted to the front head tube on all SL-70s. The tag was black with silver text. The top right corner of the tag had the month and year. Gary Lewis of Michigan arguably owns the largest pile of New Old Stock SL-70 parts in the world, and he talked about the speedometer and the horn kits as dealer add-on items that customers could purchase. These are a few of the hard to find parts today. The highest serial number reported is by Randy Marble. His serial number 1084757 makes it the 84,757th bike built of the first model SL-70s.

Original sales brochure highlighting the all-new first model SL-70 Motosport in Light Ruby Red.

Chapter 25

SL-70 K1 1973 Honda

Beginning Serial Number 1100001-1119680

The final SL-70 was produced in 1973. The final model was called the SL-70 K1. Many of the features remained the same as the previous model; however plenty of new things made the K1 the iconic motorcycle that it is today.

Three all new colors were available for '73. The buyer had the choice of Fire Red, Candy Special Yellow, and Candy Riviera Blue Special. The taillight/license plate bracket switched from chrome to black. It was not the same bracket either. The K1 bracket has three holes cut out of the top of the bracket. The taillight and taillight lens was enlarged for more visibility and were the same as the H and K1 CT-70. The sticker on the

A Fire Red model SL-70 K1 Motorsport owned by Randy Marble of Texas.

Black license plate frame and taillight bracket mounted on a metal painted rear fender in Fire Red.

SL-70 K1 in Candy Yellow Special.

fuel tank was the same for all three colors. The decal was yellow with two black stripes making a circular type of pattern around the "Honda" name. The side cover stickers were switched to a simplistic "70" sticker in yellow with a bold black outline to match the tank stickers. New for the K1 on the left side of the motorcycle just behind the rear shock on the frame was a black helmet holder. The frame had a yellow sticker with black writing commonly found on many Honda Motorcycles in the early to mid-70s that said, "helmet holder". Another addition was a fork lockset added to the front fork. It required the same key as the ignition and the helmet lock. Honda moved the front reflectors from the headlight to the fork tubes and they went with larger fork reflectors. Because the reflectors were moved, it required new fork headlight stay ears to be added as well.

Another addition for the K1 was a horn mounted between the front fork tubes just below the headlight. The left side of the handle bar had a black horn button unlike the first model that just had a plug in the bar. A standard feature on the K1 was a speedometer assembly. It was the same as the four speed HK1 CT-70. It was a pimply metal-finished body shaped like a canister with a black rubber ring around the top edge of the speedometer. The face was black with white numbers and hash marks. The speedometer topped out at fifty miles per hour instead of sixty like the previous model. The bottom of the face had a white "HM" logo signifying Honda Motor Company. Unlike the first model speedometer, this unit mounted to the lower handlebar holder under the triple tree.

The ignition switch, wire harness, and battery changed for the K1. The coil and rectifier remained the same as the previous model. The rear shocks on the K1 were different from the early shocks used on the first-model SL-70. The switch over took place at serial number 1037835 and ran until the last SL-70 K1 was produced. The second run of the shocks used on the K1 had chrome bottoms. The right side control switch was a K1 only item. The thickest portion of the red twist knob on the kill switch is at the bottom of the switch by the L/H engraving. This differs from the previous switch, which has the thickest portion pointing at the on/off side of the switch. A front brake stop switch with a gray cable plugged into the lever perch on both the first model and the K1 SL-70. The gray cables, the handlebar, the complete wheel/tire/hub assemblies were the same as the previous model. The air cleaner assembly was unique to the K1 model. It came in semi glazed black finish with chrome end caps. The rear fender had two warning labels. At the rear of the fender was a tire caution-warning sticker in black with silver text. The front of the fender had a battery caution sticker. The down tube between the rear shock and the side cover was a silver, muffler-warning decal with black text. Based on the beginning serial number and the final serial number listed for fuel tanks it appears that 19,680 SL-K1s were produced.

2nd run rear shock with chrome bottoms to match the coil springs.

Large chrome motocross style handlebars and a Fire Red headlight shell with a chrome trim ring.

Candy Riviera Blue Special fuel tank with gold and black Honda tank sticker.

Factory speedometer, a standard feature on all SL-70 K1 models.

Four-speed manual transmission clutch cover with removable center cover.

NOS SL-70 Rear Shock. Gary Lewis Collection

Right side Low/hi and on/off kill switch. Mirror mount integrated into brake lever mount.

Cloud Silver flywheel cover with removable points cover.

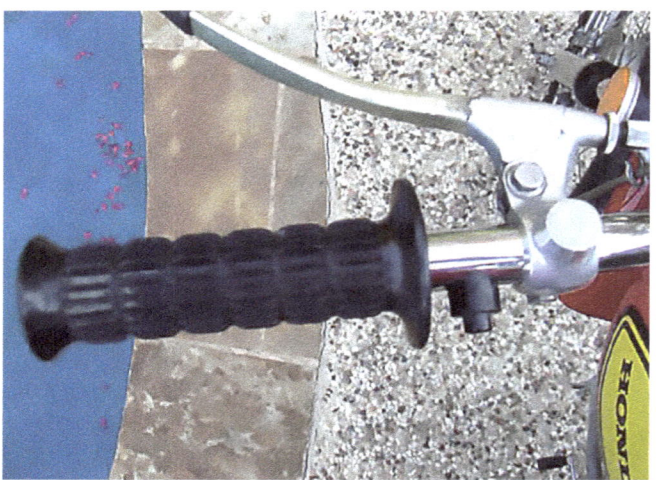

Horn button, standard equipment on all SL-70 K1 models.

Chapter 26

XL-70 Honda

Beginning Serial Number 1000001

After three calendar years of production and two models, the SL-70 line was dropped and Honda switched the line over to the XL-70. The XL-70 was produced for three model years, from 1974-1976. The engine in the XL-70 was a 72cc Overhead cam single cylinder with a four-speed manual hand clutch transmission.

The first model XL-70 to the untrained eye looked almost identical to a SL-70 K1. The XL-70 came in one color for '74, Candy Topaz Orange. Instead of a silver frame, the XL had a frame and rear swing arm painted black. A black headlight bucket rather than one to match the tank color was the style for the all-new XL-70. The headlight bucket

1974 Candy Topaz Orange XL-70 owned by Randy Marble.

Turn signals were standard equipment in 1974 on the XL-70.

was the same as the ones used on all K1-1979 CT-70s. The speedometer was a carryover from the last model SL-70 K1. The speedometer housing was silver with a black rubber trim ring. The face was black with white numbers and hash marks. The bottom of the speedometer had an "HM" logo and the top left corner was a green neutral indicator light and the top right was a red high-beam indicator light. The speedometer topped out at fifty miles per hour. The foot brake pedal switched from chrome to a black pedal to match the frame for the all-new XL. The gas tank had a black stripe along the top with a bold black stripe accompanied by a pin stripe in the front portion of the tank. The side of the tank had a black "Honda" logo outlined in white. The side covers said "XL70" in black with a white outline.

The muffler remained the same as the SL-70. The taillight/license plate bracket was exclusive to the first model as well as the XL-70 K1 and like many of the components; it too came in black paint. The taillight was the same as the last model SL-70. A chrome handlebar was used on the first model XL and it was exclusive to this model only. The fork bridge used was the same as the last model SL-70, it was only used on the first model XL-70, and it came in Cloud Silver. The first model XL-70 used the same aluminum handlebar risers found on both models of the SL-70. A new feature added to the bottom two bolts of the bar risers was the turn signal pilot lamp assembly to let the rider know the turn signals were on and flashing. An all-new handgrip was used on the XL-70. It was black rubber with horizontal ribbed lines and large donuts. A semi-gloss black air cleaner assembly was used on the first two model XL-70s as well as the final SL-70 model. The seat used on the XL-70 was the same as the last model SL-70 and it was a one-year only seat in the XL-70 lineup.

Like some other parts on the first year XL, the rear shocks used were the same as those used on the late model SL-70 K1. The shocks had chrome coil springs with chrome lowers and clear-coated aluminum uppers. Perhaps the biggest and most noticeable feature on the XL-70, when compared to the SL-70 lineup, is the addition of turn signals. Chrome arms mounted to the front headlight ears and chrome bezels with round amber plastic lenses gave onlookers a visible indicator that the rider wanted to make a right or left turn. The rear signals mounted to the rear chrome grab bar. The front fork legs were the same as the last model SL-70 with the large round reflectors. Just like the SL-70, the XL-70s used a 44-tooth rear

Aluminum turn signal and horn switch. Accordion black rubber lever covers.

Aluminum low/hi kill switch assembly.

Candy Topaz plastic side cover with a black and white XL 70 sticker.

Black frame, chrome shifter, and Cloud Silver flywheel cover with removable points cover.

sprocket and a 92-link chain.

The chrome wheels with spokes and the two and half by sixteen front tires and the two and three quarter by fourteen inch, rear tires were the same as the SL-70 and SL-70 K1. Honda kept things simple when it came to carburation, kickers, and shifters; they used the same carburetor as well as kickers and shifters on all SL-70s and XL-70s. The rear bumper in chrome, however is exclusive to the XL-70 lineup and it was used on all three models. The lever mounting brackets with mirror mounts were the same as the ones used on the SL-70s. The left and right control switches however were unique to the first model XL-70. The left side switch was aluminum with a black turn signal control switch. The right side switch was aluminum and came with a red on/off kill switch twist knob, and a black low and high beam control slide switch at the bottom of the housing. The right side switch also housed the throttle tube and cable and this was a one-year only set-up as well for the XL-70.

The hand brake levers remained the same as the SL-70, however to the untrained eye the addition of the accordion black lever covers gave them a whole new look and helped keep dirt out and preserve the cables. The clutch and front brake cables came in gray and remained the same as the SL-70. The throttle cable also came in gray and was used on the SL-70 as well as all XL-70s up to frame number 1012635. The clutch and flywheel magneto covers remained the same as the SL-70s. The kickstand changed to black for the XL-70, to match the frame. The horn remained the same as the one used on the SL-70s. Because the only color offered was Candy Topaz Orange, the front fender bracket was exclusive to the first model XL-70. The front and rear fenders, like the tank and the side cover, came in Candy Topaz Orange. The chain guard came in semi-gloss black, just like the SL-70s.

Even though the frame was black, the rear brake stopper arm remained the same as the SL-70s and came in silver. Concerning the electrical system on the all-new XL-70, several items changed from the SL-70. The wire harness changed with the addition of the turn signals. Like many motorcycles of the time period, the rectifier was changed to a silicon type and it was produced by the Shindengen Company of Japan. The ignition coil was unique to the XL-70 line and stayed the same for all three years. A different battery tray as well as battery was used. The battery was a 6N4C-1B. The ignition switch used on the XL-70 was the same

Chrome rear grab bar with turn signal mounts.

Black taillight bracket with license plate frame. Candy Topaz Orange metal rear fender with tire caution sticker.

Large coil spring rear shocks in chrome. Semi-gloss black chain guard like the SL-70.

as the last model SL-70. The front fork lock was keyed the same as the ignition switch. This was the same fork lock as that used by the SL-70 K1. The stickers used on the XL-70 were the following: A white text on a clear background "remember to preserve nature-always wear a helmet-think safety," sticker was placed on top of the fuel tank just below the gas cap. A yellow with black text "helmet holder" sticker was placed just below the helmet lock on the down-tube of the frame. A tire caution sticker, black with silver text, was applied to the rear of the fender. A battery caution sticker was also applied to the fender. A silver muffler-warning sticker with black text was present on the downtube between the right side cover and the rear shock.

Candy Topaz Orange and Black fuel tank with flat chrome cap. Honda sticker in black, outlined in white, and black.

Chapter 27

Honda XL-70 K1

Beginning serial number 1100003

After one year of production, Honda presented the world with an improved version of the XL-70, the XL-70 K1. Like the previous model, Honda only offered one color, Candy Riviera Blue Special for 1975. For the first time in SL-70 and XL-70 history Honda went with a painted fender color that differed from the main body kit color. This time the fenders were painted "Special Silver Metallic". Another new feature was the rear shocks. They went from chrome coils to black painted coils. The uppers and lowers remained metal finished rather than black. The handlebar used was a one-year only item along with the handlebar risers, and the throttle cable. The fork bridge, bar

1975 XL-70 K1 in Candy Riviera Blue Special owned by Randy Marble.

Wide Motocross chrome bars with black bar risers, triple clamp, and cables.

risers, and the turn signal indicator bracket all came in black. The grips, turn signal pilot lamp assembly, and the fork top bridge in semi-glazed black were carryover items from the first model Xl-70. The wire harness, battery, silicon rectifier, ignition switch, and coil were used on the previous model XL as well. The foot pegs underwent a change from the previous model. They went from fold up pegs with rubber, to black painted fold up steel foot pegs with teeth to insure good footing, even in wet conditions. The kickstand came in black and a new feature for 1975 was the stand-rubber. The rear brake rod and rear brake switch remained the same as the previous model, however the footbrake pedal was changed for the K1 and it remained black in color. Parts that carried over from the preceding year include the front forks, and the air cleaner. However, the housing side covers were black instead of chrome. The fuel tank received the new paint color, Candy Riviera Blue Special and it also received a new sticker for each side. The new sticker was a gold Honda wing with black detail lines and the word Honda below it in white, outlined in black. The side covers matched the tank; however, they received new stickers as well. The sticker said "XL" in red, outlined in white with a black background. Below, it said "70" in white outlined in black.

Black components seemed to be the common theme with the K1. The handlebar controls were black and the configuration of the controls changed from the previous model. The left side switch had the high/low light switch up top and the turn signal left-and-right switch at the bottom. The right side switch assembly had a red on/off twist knob for the kill switch. New for the K1 was a small black bracket that mounted next to the kill switch and the donut end of the grip to house the throttle tube and the throttle cable. The cables were black and the throttle cable had a rubber dust cover where it plugged into the mount on the handlebar. Another new feature is the seat. The seat went from a black pebble grain vinyl, with nine, heat pressed seams along the top, to a mild grain seat with no pattern on the top of the cover. The rear of the cover had pipping that went at an angle before wrapping around the top edge of the seat. The back of the seat had the signature "Honda" logo in silver. The rest of the components remained the same as the previous model year. Randy Marble of Texas restored serial number 1104204. Less than 5,000 1975 K1 were produced and like most classic motorcycles, it remains difficult to find one in nice original condition.

Metal rear fender in Special Silver Metallic paint. Black license plate and taillight bracket.

Black metal headlight bucket with chrome trim ring. Chrome fork uppers with chrome turn signal brackets. Metal front fender in Special Silver Metallic paint.

Cloud Silver flywheel cover with removable points cover with Honda text outlined in black.

Chrome rear grab bar with rear turn signal mounts.

Black on/off kill switch assembly. A new throttle set-up for 1975.

Black exhaust system and aluminum rear hubs with spoke wheels.

Hi/low and left-and-right control switch.

Black vinyl seat without ribs on top of the cover. Candy Riviera Blue Special side cover with XL 70 emblem.

Chapter 28

Honda XL-70 K2

Beginning Serial Number 1200003

For 1976, Honda dropped the K model name and started going by the year of production. The final XL-70, like the previous model, underwent subtle styling changes, but it remained the same motorcycle. True to form, only one color was produced for the final XL-70. Collectors know this color as Mighty Green; however, the Honda sales brochure refers to it by Solid Green. Other than the color, very little changed with the '76 XL-70. The most noticeable changes were the color of the taillight bracket, which went from black to silver to match the fenders. The side cover stickers also made a color change. Each side cover sticker had a large "XL" in yellow with a black background boarder. Below was "70" in white with a black background boarder. The MX-type, slim, heavily padded seat

Mighty Green/Solid Green 1976 XL-70 K2 owned by Randy Marble.

remained the same as the previous model year. As did the rear shocks with five adjustable positions to give the rider just the ride he or she wanted. Remaining features stayed the same as the previous model year. The headlight, taillight, turn signals, and the ability to go on and off road are what made the XL-70 unique. After three short model years, XL-70 production ceased. Randy Marble freshened up a '76 XL-70 and commented about the rarity of finding one of these last-model bikes. The serial number is 1204193 making it the 4,193rd XL produced. No production numbers have been reported. However, based on other small motorcycles of the time like the CT-70, it certainly was below 10,000 units.

Chrome rear grab handle with turn signal mounts. Taillight bracket and rear fender colors matched for 1976.

A separate headlight and speedometer were standard on all XL-70s. Large chrome motocross bars.

Black frame, black air cleaner with black side covers, and chrome kick starter arm. Large alligator fold-up foot pegs.

Books from Wolfgang Publications can be found at many book stores and numerous web sites.

Titles	ISBN	Price	# of pages
Advanced Airbrush Art	9781929133208	$29.95	144 pages
Advanced Custom Motorcycle Assembly & Fabrication	9781929133239	$29.95	144 pages
Advanced Custom Motorcycle Wiring - *Revised*	9781935828761	$29.95	144 pages
Advanced Pinstripe Art	9781929133321	$29.95	144 pages
Advanced Sheet Metal Fab	9781929133123	$29.95	144 pages
Advanced Tattoo Art - *Revised*	9781929133822	$29.95	144 pages
Airbrush How-To with Mickey Harris	9781929133505	$29.95	144 pages
Building Hot Rods	9781929133437	$29.95	144 pages
Colorful World of Tattoo Models	9781935828716	$34.95	144 pages
Composite Materials 1	9781929133765	$29.95	144 pages
Composite Materials 2	9781929133932	$29.95	144 pages
Composite Materials 3	9781935828662	$29.95	144 pages
Composite Materials Step by Step Projects	9781929133369	$29.95	144 pages
Cultura Tattoo Sketchbook	9781935828839	$32.95	284 pages
Custom Bike Building Basics	9781935828624	$24.95	144 pages
Custom Motorcycle Fabrication	9781935828792	$29.95	144 pages
Harley-Davidson Sportster Hop-Up & Customizing Guide	9781935828952	$29.95	144 pages
Harley-Davidson Sportser Buell Engine Hop-Up Guide	9781929133093	$27.95	144 pages
Harley-Davidson Twin Cam-Hop Up	9781929133697	$29.95	144 pages
Harley-Davidson Evo Hop-Up/Build	9781941064337	$29.95	144 pages
How Airbrushes Work	9781929133710	$24.95	144 pages
Honda Enthusiast Guide Motorcycles 1959-1985	9781935828853	$29.95	144 pages
Honda Mini Trail	9781941064320	$29.95	144 pages
How-To Airbrush, Pinstripe & Goldleaf	9781935828693	$29.95	144 pages
How-To Build Old Skool Bobber - 2nd Edition	9781935828785	$29.95	144 pages

 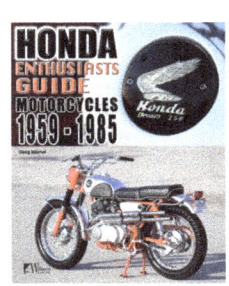 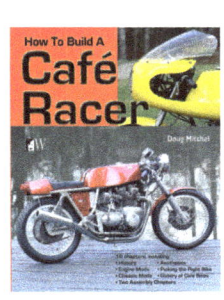  

Books from Wolfgang Publications can be found at many book stores and numerous web sites.

Titles	ISBN	Price	# of pages
How-To Build a Cheap Chopper	9781929133178	$29.95	144 pages
How-To Build Cafe Racer	9781935828730	$29.95	144 pages
How-To Chop Tops	9781929133499	$24.95	144 pages
How-To Fix American V-Twin	9781929133727	$29.95	144 pages
How-To Paint Tractors & Trucks	9781929133475	$29.95	144 pages
Hot Rod Wiring	9781929133987	$29.95	144 pages
Hot Rod Chassis How-To	9781929133703	$29.95	144 Pages
Kosmoski's *New* Kustom Paint Secrets	9781929133833	$29.95	144 pages
Learning the English Wheel	9781935828891	$29.95	144 pages
Mini Ebooks - Butterfly and Roses	9781935828167	Ebook Only	
Mini Ebooks - Skulls & Hearts	9781935828198	Ebook Only	
Mini Ebooks - Lettering & Banners	9781935828204	Ebook Only	
Mini Ebooks - Tribal Stars	9781935828211	Ebook Only	
Power Hammers	9781929133604	$29.95	144 pages
Pro Pinstripe	9781929133925	$29.95	144 pages
Sheet Metal Bible	9781929133901	$29.95	176 pages
Sheet Metal Fab Basics B&W	9781929133468	$24.95	144 pages
Sheet Metal Fab for Car Builders	9781929133383	$29.95	144 pages
SO-CAL Speed Shop, Hot Rod Chassis	9781935828860	$29.95	144 pages
Tattoo Bible #1	9781929133840	$29.95	144 pages
Tattoo Bible #2	9781929133857	$29.95	144 pages
Tattoo Bible #3	9781935828754	$29.95	144 pages
Tattoo Lettering Bible	9781935828921	$29.95	144 pages
Tattoo Sketchbook, Jim Watson	9781935828037	$32.95	112 pages
Triumph Restoration - Pre Unit	9781929133635	$29.95	144 pages
Triumph Restoration - Unit 650cc	9781929133420	$29.95	144 pages
Vintage Dirt Bikes - Enthusiast's Guide	9781929133314	$29.95	144 pages
Ultimate Sheet Metal Fab	9780964135895	$24.95	144 pages
Ultimate Triumph Collection	9781935828655	$49.95	144 pages

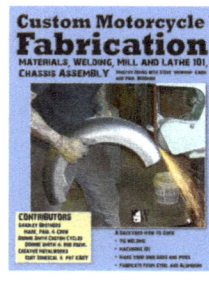

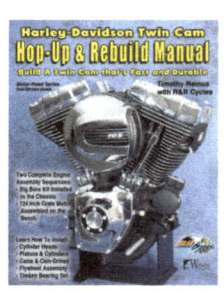
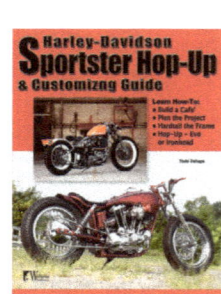

www.ingramcontent.com/pod-product-compliance
Lightning Source LLC
Chambersburg PA
CBHW041242240426
43668CB00025B/2462